Pareto Principle

Unleash the True Power of the Pareto Principle

(The Secret Strategy to Optimizing Every Area of Your Life)

Joanne Carver

Published By **Zoe Lawson**

Joanne Carver

Pareto Principle: Unleash the True Power of the Pareto Principle (The Secret Strategy to Optimizing Every Area of Your Life)

ISBN 978-1-998769-37-7

Legal & Disclaimer

medical advice before using any of the suggested remedies, techniques, or information in this book.

Upon using the information contained in this book, you agree to hold harmless the Author from and against any damages, costs, and expenses, including any legal fees potentially resulting from the application of any of the information provided by this guide. This disclaimer applies to any damages or injury caused by the use and application, whether directly or indirectly, of any advice or information presented, whether for breach of contract, tort, negligence, personal injury, criminal intent, or under any other cause of action.

You agree to accept all risks of using the information presented inside this book. You need to consult a professional medical practitioner in order to ensure you are both able and healthy enough to participate in this program.

Table of contents

Chapter 1: The Laws of Success

Succession is a common trait

What is the secret to success? Do they have the ability to grasp complex concepts quickly and easily? Is success a pure time management question? Or does success depend on many factors?

You can have success in many forms. While some people define success in financial terms, others see it as personal experiences or feelings. However you define success, there is one thing that will remain constant: success is subjective. To be successful, you do not need to compare yourself to other people. To succeed, you have to follow your heart and your intuition. Only you can decide if and to what degree you are successful. Only you know if your success or failure.

However, if your goal is to copy the success of others and be like them, you will not succeed in life. Only then can you determine what success is important to you and be able do your best work towards it.

These seven characteristics are the hallmarks of many successful people.

1. You must have a strong work ethic. Hard work has been the only way to get to where you are today. The only way to be successful is to work hard. People you look up too have invested thousands of time in their talents and made great use of them. Not all people are equally talented. Some people are more intelligent than others. Every person has unique strengths and weaknesses. A successful person is able to recognize their strengths as well as weaknesses and assess the potential profit they could make.

Work ethic training is a great way to get more out your life. Setting a personal goal to motivate yourself is the best way to do this. It is also important to shift your perspective on work. The job is only a tool for personal success. When you understand the reasons you work, you'll do your best to maximize your work and get as much done as possible. It is possible to improve your work ethic by surrounding oneself with people who work hard than you. It is no surprise that many people over time are believed to acquire character traits from five of their closest friends. People who are highly motivated and have a strong work ethic will help you develop a work ethic. You will see a faster process if you spend more time around these people.

People who take on more responsibility also tend to have a stronger work ethic. You will be more responsible if you have the responsibility to look after others. It is important to not take on more responsibility that you can handle. You will be more productive if you find yourself in this position. Try to be the person who takes responsibility. You will see lasting improvements in your work ethics and approach to work if you do this.

Get feedback from other people about your work. It's a good feeling to be praised by someone and that will encourage you to work harder. Negative feedback is possible. Negative feedback can be difficult to handle. Negative feedback is more helpful than personal attacks. You should see such feedback as a benefit and take steps to implement it.

One can summarize that success is directly connected to a lot of hard work. People who do not love their work will likely not have found a motivating goal. You can't improve your work ethic faster than it takes. It is essential to accept that the process will take time in order for it to be sustainable.

2. A vision and precise goals: You'll never again question why you are working on a project. This helps you stay on track and increases your self-confidence. Achieving

success requires that you have clear goals. Get clear about your vision. This vision, or long term goal, should only be possible in the next few years. If this is your definition success, you can set yourself the challenge to travel to all countries in the world. You could also make it a goal to make money. This vision should be divided into small goals. If you have a financial goal, then you can try to earn a certain amount each month. You will reach your long term goal if you are able to accumulate this amount over a longer span of time. It is a good idea to break down big goals into smaller ones. Only take the steps necessary to reach your goal. Doing this will help you transform a goal that seemed impossible at first glance into an achievable goal.

Your goals should be precise in order to achieve them. Your goal should be written down. You should then make your goals concrete. Perhaps you could assign a value to your goal. If your goal is to travel the world, it could be the number and locations of all the countries. If your goal involves money, you might define a budget to achieve your goal. Once you have established a measurable goal, you should consider whether the goal is feasible. Is your goal realistic? If so, can you really achieve it. You can test drive your goal and see if it is achievable in one week. If you meet your week's goals, it is likely that your goal was achievable.

The penultimate step should be to ensure that your goal truly has personal meaning. Success is subjective. This was explained at the beginning. You define success, and you decide whether or not you succeed. If you think success is what other people have, you may be lacking motivation to achieve your goal. Only when you truly know what you want, you can set goals that are worth pursuing.

We also need to set a timeframe in order for the goal to be achieved. What time should it take before you achieve the big, long-term goal. How long does it take to achieve all of your smaller goals along the path to the big long-term objective? It is important to set time limits for the achievement of both small and large goals. Sometimes you can define a goal, but you don't get to achieve it because you haven't given a time frame.

3. A good time manager will help you make progress quickly. Understanding the concept of time is essential to better manage your time. A successful person will know how crucial time management is. Effective time management and efficiency are crucial building blocks to your own success. Not only should you ensure you are efficient in your work and keep on top of your tasks, but you must also be effective and efficient with your time.

You can start by being more aware of the time you spend. You can give it a financial value. An hour of work could be compared to an hour with friends. This will show you how important your time really is, and encourage you to do better with it than working. Succession is a realization that time is finite. Money can be earned or spent. You can't earn time. It is impossible to get time back once it is gone. Recognize this fact. This will make it easier to manage your time effectively.

For example, the Pomodoro Technique can be used to maximize your time management at workplace. This is how the Pomodoro technique works: You work in two shifts of twenty five to five. The first twenty-five-minute work period is followed by a five-minute rest. During these twenty five minutes, you need to be as focused and unaffected as possible. Take a five minute break from work to do something that distracts you completely and clears your mind.

The two minute rule can be used to quickly eliminate unwanted tasks. The rule stipulates that you must complete all tasks in less than 2 minutes. Do you need to make a phone call that you don't like? It's not too late. Is it not your intention to write an e mail? Now, write it. Are you feeling like answering important texts? Do it right now if the task takes you less that two minutes.

You can also use A-B/C to organize your tasks. Divide your tasks into B, C and A tasks. A task should be done as soon as you can. This should be your highest priority. B tasks are tasks which you may not need to complete immediately, but should be completed soon. The C tasks are tasks that can be completed in a reasonable time and have no priority. Once you've completed class A, distribute your tasks across these classes. Then, work at full speed on Class B and then C.

4. Motivation is temporary. Discipline lasts. Motivation is not possible. Discipline can be learned. The key to long-term success is discipline. It is easy to give up on your goals after you have worked hard towards them.

It is important to be persistent, to not lose heart, and to work hard.

Modifying your work style can make it easier to maintain discipline. People stop working on a task if they do not want to. An organized person will stop working once the task has been completed. You need to be able to put aside any preconceived notions and stop working on them.

Setting specific times to work can help you improve your discipline. Your goal is to start work at 09.00 today. The first step will make it easier to follow the others. Once you get started working, you will see that it is not that bad and that it was not something you had to avoid.

Setting goals is an important part of self-discipline. Your objective is what you set for yourself. Set a pace that allows you to tackle each goal one by one. Don't get discouraged.

You need to minimize distractions if you want to be productive and disciplined. Distractions can be your smartphone or other devices, but you may also spend too much time with people who don't support you. This could hinder your ability to achieve your goals. It is important to limit distractions while working. Your productivity and ability to pursue your dreams more effectively will result in more time available for you to enjoy other activities.

5. Confidence: A person who views themselves negatively about themselves is less likely to be successful in their pursuits. Many people struggle with low self-confidence. People who look up to you are usually people who had to struggle with self-confidence in the past and have rebuilt it.

To improve your self confidence, the first step is to recognize what is stopping you from improving it. It is also important to identify the reasons you lack self-confidence.

Practice is the best way for self-confidence to be built. Although the theory may sound interesting, it is rarely true. Self-confidence can only be built if you step outside your comfort zone and are willing to challenge yourself. Fear is the main obstacle to you succeeding in such an environment. People avoid difficult situations because they fear making mistakes or embarrassment. Learning is only possible through mistakes. Every person you look up has either made a fool or is afraid to get into similar situations. You can't stay in your comfort zone.

Your goals will help boost your self-confidence. If you do something important to yourself, you'll quickly gain respect. It's important to not only work on your inner self, but also on the outside. You must work on your body language. Don't hide it from anyone. Get into a posture that is more comfortable and don't cross your arms.

In addition to your posture, it is important to note your successes. Our inner voice often tells our minds that we are not good enough, or that we will fail. If you meticulously record your successes, it will be easy to prove to yourself that they are real. Take, for example, a list that you keep track of your successes. You should also date them.

6. Strategy is crucial for success at work and in private life. Some people seem to have the right strategies for every situation. Others don't have them at all. Expertise in your field is the key to success. It is important to have a good understanding of the specific area in which you work to create the right strategy. This knowledge will enable you to evaluate the situation better and create potential solutions.

7. Implementation is key. A strategy is great, but it's only half the battle. A successful person doesn't think but does the work. While everyone has ideas, and everybody

can think of good things, few people actually implement their plans. Do not rejoice over potential strategies or ideas, but only be happy when they have been implemented. It is essential to understand yourself and to assess your abilities if you wish to achieve success. You can only determine where your performance limits are and then you will know what goals you can achieve.

It is impossible to break success down into a handful of factors. However, there are similarities between successful people. It is okay to not be able to apply the above factors. There are always exceptions. And success is such a subjective concept that it is difficult to pinpoint the characteristics and abilities of a successful person. You can be you and not pretend to to be someone else. But, try to become the best version possible of yourself.

Why few people are successful

There are many reasons people fail to succeed. People don't succeed because they lack the right education, financial status, family situation or motivation.

As we've seen, many people aren't even ready to define what success looks like. Do you define success as driving beautiful cars or having a partner? Or maximizing your personal freedom and independence? Whatever success means to YOU, it must be defined. The sooner you can define success, the quicker you'll be successful.

Many people are not successful because of their circumstances. But, they also give up too easily. Successful people have had to deal with difficult situations and pushed themselves beyond their limits. It's easy to underestimate how hard it can be for someone to succeed, especially if their path has not been marked. Many people feel disappointed in themselves and say they will never succeed.

Successful people do something no other person would be willing to do. To discover what is holding your success back, ask the following questions:

* What issues are currently affecting your life?

* Which are your most frustrating failures?

* How do I define my personal goals?

* Are your talents being fully utilized? If not, what is the reason?

* What distractions keep you from focusing on your goals?

* What are the tasks you're not currently completing that you should be? These tasks are not possible.

* Do you like your job? If so, why is that?

* Are You Happy with Yourself?

* Do you feel in control or do others determine your situation?

* Are your goals achievable if you are disciplined?

Take a note of the results. It is likely that there are still inner conflicts that stop you from succeeding. These inner conflicts must be overcome in order to succeed and make the most out of your time.

Five laws that guarantee success for everyone

The laws that lead to success are what we'll be discussing in the coming weeks. Here are five laws that can be applied to this topic.

1. Be true to yourself: What strengths do you possess and when can you utilize them? Focusing on your weaknesses is what many people do. It is more beneficial to look at your strengths rather than dwell on your flaws. There are ways to get around your weaknesses. It is possible to outsource weak points. It is the same for your personal skills. If you don't know how to do something or it takes you months of practice, outsourcing it

will be a better option. If you can rely on your strengths, then you will excel at something and be able achieve unimaginable success. If you don't depend on your strengths, it will be difficult to make yourself valuable to others, such employers or business contacts.

2. Focus on your effectiveness, not your competition. The race is won by those who work harder and smarter. You must ensure that your work methods produce the best results. Examine your competitors to see what they have done well, which strategies worked and which methods are most effective. Learn from your competition until you're better than your rivals. It can be an motivating force in your life. It's not surprising that competition can stimulate the market. It is therefore a good idea to have competitors.

3. Never dwell on past errors: There are always things that went wrong. Everyone makes mistakes. You must learn from your

errors. There will be many mistakes made in your career. However, there will be other mistakes that are not obvious and that you shouldn't waste any time pondering about. Only one thing is important is to not repeat your mistakes. Learn from your mistakes and you'll make fewer mistakes the next time. There are worse things than repeating the same mistakes. If you make a mistake, you should reflect on it and consider what you could have done differently next time. Once you've made this determination, you can move on to the next step and stop worrying about it.

People who don't reflect on their mistakes and fail to make amends will continue to fail. It is easy to glorify failure and think that every misstep is a blessing. This is often false. There are certain mistakes that you should avoid and which can make it difficult to recover. It is important to correct any mistakes quickly so that you don't make them again.

4. Learn more every single day: Make an effort to learn new things every day. You can do this by watching videos online, reading books, speaking with other people, or practicing your skills. Learning is a key to success. It helps you avoid common mistakes and increases your chances of success. Find opportunities to learn. Are you looking for a great online course? Are there any courses at universities you could take? Are there any recommended readings? Whatever your choice, be open to learning something new. Look for the application of what your learning will lead you to. How can you use your new skills at work, or with friends? What will it be like for you to acquire these skills and what personal goals can they help you reach?

5. Don't be content with your achievements: Anyone who rests too long on their laurels will fail. There is no successful person I know who has settled down on their laurels. Many people who succeed are constantly looking

for new opportunities to get better, richer and more successful. If you stop looking for the next opportunity, it will be difficult to get back on track and continue working towards your goals. It is normal to celebrate achievements and give yourself a high five. However, if you believe you can just relax after first successes, you will find yourself in a rut. It is a long-term process that requires you to work hard and put in time. However, if you are willing do it, you can always celebrate your success.

Chapter 2: The Pareto principle in history

Introduction to Pareto principle

Pareto is a time management system that can be applied in different situations. The Pareto principle is a time management method that gives you a ratio of 80 to 20. Twenty percent of work can often make a difference in professional success. Different methods of working are therefore more productive than others. Recognizing this and taking the Pareto principle as its word will help you improve your time management.

The Pareto Principle allows us to focus our efforts on the most productive strategies to increase productivity. Pareto can be used to help save time and shape your work. This not only saves time, but it also allows one to make more progress. One can spend less time working towards a goal and still achieve the same result. Knowing the right strategies to use to succeed will help you stand out against your competition and get a head start.

However, those who continue to ignore the Pareto Principle and only focus on the twenty-five percent of the methods that yield the best results will fall behind and be unable to make any progress. Concentrating on the twenty% of methods leading to eighty% of the results will allow you to work five times faster mathematically than someone who also concentrates on the eighty% that lead to twenty% of the results.

Pareto's principle states that success is possible by working less. Twenty percent are achieved in only eighty percent work hours. Eighty percent are achieved in only twenty percent. If you want to do less work and are happy with only eighty percent, you should perform the twenty per cent of the tasks that lead you to eighty% of your results. This strategy results in a reduction of five percent and a decrease in the amount one achieves. This strategy helps people reduce their working hours while allowing them to have more time for other activities.

Pareto is a principle that can help you manage your time better. You'll soon notice it in every aspect of your life. This concept is built into all things if you pay more attention to the environment around you. Only people who can understand it will be able to use it to their benefit.

Vilfredo Pareto is the inventor of the Pareto Principle

Pareto principles are not the idea of a time-management coach. They are a well-known concept that has been understood and applied for more than 100 years. Vilfredo Pereto, a sociologist and economist, was the one who developed the Pareto principle. He did this when he studied how wealth distribution in Italy at the start of the twentieth century.

Pareto's work on the criticism of ideological phenomena, his sociological works and his sociological works are just a few of the many things that made him famous. He also worked in the fields psychology and economy. Pareto's distribution, Pareto optimum, and Pareto diagram were also named for him.

Pareto is still an important writer on the topic of revolution, evolution and rationalism (in a political setting).

It is not known that Pareto did not view the Pareto rule as an eighty-to-20y ratio. His view was that any ratio could work, not just the 80/20 ratio. As an example, thirty per cent of the work could yield sixty percent of its results. A ratio of eighty-20 is acceptable.

People also believe that the sum of one-hundred percent, which is in the eighty to twenty proportion, must be reached. This is a common misconception. This misconception can be dispelled by assuming that a hundred percent of the results are achieved using one hundred per cent of the working hours.

Justification for Pareto principle

These ratios can all be found in nature, if one is willing to look closely. While the eighty/twenty ratio helps with time management and productivity, it can also be used to describe other situations.

Pareto only describes. The ratio of bicycle accidents caused by cyclists would be 75% if this was the case. The same holds true for any other situation in life.

But, to be able justify the Pareto rule without error, we need to make sure that parts of a system are not interdependent. It is therefore essential that there be no interdependence of the parts. It is possible to say that time, work, and accidents involving bicycles are not interdependent.

Pareto principles are only meant to describe a situation. They have logical limitations. For example, it is impossible to complete ninety per cent of tasks in one hundred and fifty percent of the time. A hundred percent can also not cause accident zero percent.

Chapter 3: Pareto principle

Pareto principle to be applied

Pareto principles can be applied in many situations. In this section of the guide, we will concentrate on the eighty to twentyy ratio. This ratio can be used for time management as well as increasing productivity. To apply this concept, you should know these three steps.

1. Twenty percent tasks - What twenty percent are the tasks that make up eighty% of the results? Make a list listing all the tasks you need to accomplish each week. This could end up being a long list. When you have completed all the tasks, prioritize them. They can be broken down into important and less important. Don't do any of these tasks. You might also consider outsourcing some tasks. Some tasks are not urgent and might only be on your mind because they require attention. It is important to ask yourself which tasks you are most concerned about and whether or

not you feel comfortable working alone. Once you have divided your tasks into important and non-important tasks, you will see that even tasks that sound urgent are not important and don't have a high priority in you life. Now you have to separate the important tasks from the less important and narrow down the tasks that will contribute to your success to 80 percent. Once you've identified the most important tasks, you can move onto the next step.

2. Create to-dos lists: Once your eighty percent are identified, you can move them to a to do list. As we have said, it is important to clearly define and follow a schedule for your tasks. You should clearly define the time you will finish the tasks, and give an example of what your expected result.

To-do lists must be as precise as possible. You can create multiple lists to track the tasks you have. To illustrate, you might create a task list for today, but also keep another list to track your tasks. This allows you to plan your week and month. It is important to test if you can meet your needs and reach the goals that you set. Sometimes you can become too optimistic and overcomplicate your tasks, forgetting that your day only has 24 hours. It is important to be realistic with yourself and challenge your limits. One way to test your to-dos list is to align your life around it for a few working days. If you discover that your to do lists are not achieving the results you want, you might revise them and run another test. If you are able to do this, then you can begin the actual work. Be willing to push yourself and be more productive every day.

3. Increase motivation: After you have created a to do list and identified important tasks, you need to think about what motivates your to accomplish these tasks. After a few productive productive days, you will find that your body is telling you that

you don't need to work as hard anymore. If you don't have a compelling reason to work hard you won't. Find something you can personally benefit from. Which company or organization do you work for Are you working towards a personal dream or a career? Do you want more freedom, or a financial goal. Whatever your goal, visualize it in the form a photo or an object you can carry around with you. That reminds you why every day you are working on your to-dos.

What does the Pareto principle mean for productivity?

Pareto principle can help you assess the importance of tasks and determine which ones are not. This will lead to increased productivity. It is possible to identify the things you need to do in order to reach your goals and also what you don't.

Many people feel like work is eating away at them. You can work every day and still not make it to the top. You don't make any progress. This is one reason many people are dissatisfied about their job. However, this is also true for everyday situations. Many of us exercise at least once a week. While we may exercise, we lose very little weight. You start to wonder why you go to so much trouble for so little. The frustration starts to set in and you quit going to the fitness center. You might be able to see all the strategies that will help you move forward.

The Pareto Principle allows us to determine which methods are effective and which do not. Three reasons why Pareto principles make you more productive

1. You focus on the important tasks. It is possible to understand how Pareto works by focusing on the 20 percent of tasks that are most effective and then concentrating on the remaining eighty percent. The remaining eighty per cent are ignored. This mindset can be applied to many aspects of life.

People who understand the Pareto Principle will be able apply it immediately to make their lives easier.

2. You work more selectively. This is false. This is because if you try to do too many things at once, you'll find it difficult to complete them all in a timely manner. Pareto could again be an answer in this situation. It is easier to focus on the most important tasks and work less at once. You will have less stress and will be able do more work.

3. Work-life balance This allows you work less and to spend more time doing what you enjoy. This could result in you being able to spend more time at home with your family, your hobby, or doing nothing. People often feel stressed out at work, and they wish there was a better work-life balance. This is what the Pareto principle allows you to achieve.

Pareto is an effective way to be more productive. However, this principle demands that you remain focused on your work and strive to do your best everyday. You must remember that only twenty percent are the tasks that will make up the eighty% of your results. This is often a difficult task. You may find yourself doing tasks that yield twenty percent of the desired results. It's important that you take an objective look at how you work and find ways to improve it. Only then will you be able use the Pareto Principle to its fullest potential for your purposes. Try to be honest with you and learn from your mistakes.

Living life according To the Pareto principle

Here are ten steps to help you align your life with Pareto principles.

1. Get to know you: It is important to understand yourself in order to be able and able to use the Pareto principle to guide

your life. Also, you should learn how to evaluate your own stamina and ability. What is the maximum amount of work you can do in a single day? Perhaps you are overestimating your capabilities. If you are going to live your life according Pareto principles, you need to be willing to do a thorough analysis of yourself and make objective choices about yourself. This can be very exhausting and frustrating, especially when there is so much else to do. Also important are the following factors: organization and ability to work continually. If you can do both, you will have no trouble living your life according to Pareto principles.

2. Identify twenty percent of the daily tasks that are most important in your life and lead to eighty per cent of the results. What are the tasks that are essential in your daily life that will result in eighty percent? As we have seen, a goal should be oriented towards a bigger goal. So make it a point to

only identify tasks that will give you value and help you advance. This will help you to keep track of your goals and accomplish your tasks. These will help you later. Do not be too meticulous when you first divide your tasks according To the Pareto principle. It is common to be wrong in the beginning. You will need time to sort your tasks and re-evaluate your goals. Only by following through with the tasks and setting goals can you be certain that the tasks are actually leading to eighty percent.

3. Reorganize your days: Now that you have set your goals and established your objectives, you need to work out how to accomplish them all in one day. What tasks will you do in the morning? At noon? In the evening? What is your level of concentration? Think about how focused you are in morning and evening. Do you prefer to work on your most important tasks immediately after you wake up, or do some things take longer?

To organize your life, identify the main things you need to do every day. What do you need to do every single day? This could be picking up your children from school. It could also be your job, or the lecture you attend every day. It could also be someone or a pet you need to take care. These are the main things that you need to remember in your new daily routine, no matter what they may be. These constants will help you to create your daily routine. Consider your own well-being and any possible problems you might encounter throughout the day. These are called variables. These variables include important phone call, emergency calls, and any activity that couldn't have been predicted. It is not possible to predict every event so you need to give yourself some breathing room.

You can write down your daily plan and then live according to it. You have the option to make any changes and change your daily routine if you need them.

4. Keep a list of your goals. What goal do you aim to achieve in one year? Pareto principles require that you be focused on results if you want to live a life of integrity. Pareto can help you manage your time better, but it is up to you to choose how to use that time. Keep track of the things you want to accomplish in the next weeks or months. Also mark the days that you aren't able to reach your goals. These days could be Christmas, mother's day or holidays. Don't assume that you can work all year round, even if you plan to.

5. Take one hour per week to assess your progress. In order to live life in accordance with the Pareto principle you should monitor your own progress. This is because you want the best possible results in the most time. One hour per week is a good time to reflect on how you can improve your work processes and whether certain tasks might be outsourced. Make sure you're maintaining the 80/20 ratio. Can you

turn twenty percent off your work time into eighty per cent of the results? While this sounds easy on paper, it's actually quite difficult in practice. It is important to measure your results to assess whether twenty percent of what you do in your workday leads to eighty% of the results. How long did it take to achieve these results through conventional methods? This is how long it took you to get these results by conventional means. You only need to do eighty percent from what you did previously. Do you think you can achieve this goal by working only twenty percent of what you normally do? If the answer is yes, you are following the Pareto principle in your life.

6. Your productivity cycles. Have ever you felt completely drained without any reason? What about days when you just can't concentrate, no matter how much you slept? These are called productivity cycles. These cycles are what every person

experiences every month. The productivity cycles that refer to mental health are different from the productivity cycles that pertain to physical health. It is possible to feel physically and mentally good on one day and be mentally exhausted and depressed on another.

These cycles can easily be measured by listening closely to your body, and recording which days you feel good. Keep a record of days when your mental state is good. This is the same for your physical cycle. You can identify the appropriate cycles by identifying the highs/lows. Now that you know when you are most productive, you can arrange your goals accordingly. Knowing that certain days are a low point in your mental health, it might make more sense not to tackle complex thinking tasks during those days. These cycles should not be considered an excuse. It is a way to get a better understanding of your productive as well as less productive phases. It's possible for these cycles to occur at different times within certain months, or even not at all. It's possible for these cycles to occur at different times or not at all. You need to adapt your daily schedule so it continues to work, even if you experience slower productivity.

7. Make your workplace pleasant. To feel motivated every day at work, it is important to make your workplace pleasant. You can take a picture of your loved ones, have a cup or tea, and feel more positive. You must feel comfortable in your workplace to be able work efficiently towards your goals.

8. Finding a balance is important: You cannot work all the time. It is essential to find a balance between your work and personal life. Find something that is both enjoyable and distracting from work. These breaks will allow you to focus on your goals and help you get back to work. You will have to take breaks every day if your break schedule is not followed. Breaks increase

concentration and productivity at work. If you become too involved in one activity or do only one thing from morning until night, you will soon lose interest and your ability to concentrate on your work.

You need to set aside time for breaks, as mentioned in the beginning. Use strategies such as the Pomodoro method or make your own rules. It is vital to understand when you are working, and when you should take breaks. It is also important to not only take one break throughout your working day, but multiple. Even if you are a very focused worker, taking a break from work every few hours can make a big difference in your productivity.

9. You can optimize your free time by using it in a way that will make you more productive at your job. It is best to not relax if you stay home from work and spend the entire evening in front the TV. Although you might feel relaxed, it is likely that you will not be able to relax for long enough to

change your mind. Many people will soon find sitting in front of the television is not relaxing. Instead, one will feel exhausted and cannot perform the services that one plans to perform the next day. Look for activities that bring you pleasure. You could get together with friends, take an excursion, or participate in sports. Find a leisure pursuit that you enjoy.

10. Seek out others who have the same attitude as you. Living your life according To the Pareto principle could lead to you becoming selfish. You must constantly examine yourself and seek out ways to improve. People around you may not have the same interests as you and might be more annoyed with you. It can be helpful to find someone with the same interests and whom you can share your ideas. You can encourage and support one another to reach your goals.

Chapter 4: Five applications of Pareto's principle

Optimization of your time management

Pareto Principle is a time management strategy. It says that twenty percent work leads into twenty percent of results and eighty percent leads to two percent. It can help you get more done in less time, make your time more efficient and give you more time for what makes life worthwhile.

The Pareto rule is useful for identifying redundant tasks. Many people try to organize their day into small time blocks to ensure that they can complete as many tasks and as much as possible. This can often prove counterproductive. People who split their time into many smaller pieces quickly become stressed and waste lots of time switching tasks. It also reduces one's concentration, which can cause one to be less focused and work less efficiently on tasks. It is true that sometimes it is easier to do tasks impulsively by setting short time intervals. However, these tight-knit days are not good for time management. When we reduce our tasks pile, we see how many of these tasks are unnecessary. Doing so allows us to find time to do the important things in our lives. It is important to eliminate all unnecessary tasks from your day and only focus on what is truly important.

Pareto also has an impact on meetings, appointments, and any other task. We can see the absurdity of many tasks and how much time it takes to accomplish them in our work environment by applying the Pareto Principle. Do we really need to hold another meeting every week? Do I really need all of these appointments? Pareto's principle simplifies life and gives you more freedom to think and work independently. Pareto's principle can also be beneficial for your time management. You might soon find yourself not being the person who is always in meetings.

People who think more deeply will see that distractions can be addressed using the Pareto principle. It is possible to rethink your life and find the things that make up eighty per cent of your positive experiences. If you do this, you will quickly realize that instant messengers like social media and instant messaging are not part and parcel of our lives. Pareto is the best way to avoid distractions. This principle helps you see which things have meaning in life and which ones don't. It is not a good idea to have things that negatively affect you in your life.

Remember, time will control if you don't control it. It is essential that you take control of your time management and implement the Pareto principle. To improve your time management, you must first acknowledge your mistakes and look for ways to optimize them. Pareto is a principle that allows you put a ratio above a particular part of your daily life. You can identify the ratio and compare it with your goal. This will help you filter out the unnecessary tasks and identify the most important tasks. Even though you may not be able to achieve twenty percent success, it is possible to still have some important tasks. If your performance is more than eighty%, and if you have to do unnecessary tasks, then don't forget to get on with the job.

Accuracy in achieving your goals

Pareto principle advocates the assumption that 20% of the work produces eighty percent of its results. The same holds true for goals. 20% of the effort put into achieving one's goals can lead to 80 percent of the results. This understanding means that not all goals will be achieved. Because eighty percent of our well-being is dependent on just twenty percent of our goals. People who set out to achieve all their goals are often unsuccessful. It is important to consider which goals you are really interested in and which ones have no personal significance for you. It will be obvious that many of the goals you had were determined externally and were only possible because of connections made by people you admire. You can learn more about yourself by focusing on your own goals. You will find it much easier to identify what your heart truly desires and then decide what your next goals are. But if we simply try to achieve other people's goals or define any goal that makes us happy, then we will always chase an idea that isn't making us happy.

Pareto's principle allows one to learn to love and accept oneself. Pareto is also a great principle for those who want to reach their goals faster than they thought possible. Pareto also states that by reducing your goals to the things you are most interested in, you can achieve more. Consider, for example, that your goal is to become a professional at multiple sports. One might be interested in becoming a chess and baseball player while also being a footballer. It is unlikely you will be a professional at all three sports. But if you are honest with yourself, and focus on what you truly want, it is possible to tackle one thing more effectively than the three other sports. Instead of becoming a professional footballer, baseball player, and chess coach, you will be able to focus on chess and not just become a professional player. People who try too many things at once are most likely to fail. Instead, you can focus your efforts and become the best in your area.

Pareto principle can be used to help clarify the meanings of certain tasks. It is easy to get stuck in your daily grind and forget how important certain tasks truly are. Sometimes understanding is only possible if you don't complete the task.

You should not forget these three points if you want to maximize your time management based on the Pareto principle.

1. Pareto is only effective if you are able to use the time that you have earned. You can be sure that you will save lots of time when you focus on the eighty percent that result in the best results. But many forget that there is always more work to be done. You shouldn't get too excited. Instead, plan how you will achieve your goals. If you plan way too much, it is exactly what Pareto protects you from: wasting time.

Pareto can also be used to save time. It is absurd to want time saved if it is not being used for something. The Pareto principle can help you save time, but you should also consider how you can make the most of your time to make it more meaningful or useful.

2. You can't determine which tasks belong in the twenty percent of tasks that lead to 80 percent of the results. If you try to organize your daily tasks in a ratio from eighty to twenty you will find that you often assign the tasks to those tasks that you enjoy the

most. This is one of the worst mistakes you can make. If you limit your task assignment to the 20% that gives you the most satisfaction, then you're lying to yourself. You won't accomplish the goals you set. Avoid being afraid of difficult tasks. Every unpleasant task can be considered a challenge, and should be taken on board.

3. Your working methods must still have a purpose. Second glance will show that you only save time if your work methods continue to produce eighty per cent of the results. Some methods might not work anymore, or your goals and circumstances change. It is possible that you will be different tomorrow than you were today. You will also need to adapt in the future. There is no guarantee that what you do now will continue to be successful in the future. It is important that you take time once a week to reflect, analyze and improve on your past performances and goals.

Pareto principle: Everyday life

Pareto is a principle that can be found in all aspects of our daily lives. You can see the Pareto principle in everyday life. Twenty percent percent of websites are on the Internet, twenty% of drivers are involved in eighty% accidents, eighty percent wear twenty per cent clothes, and twenty percent have traffic volumes exceeding eighty percent. You can think of many more everyday situations.

The question is, how do you deal with Pareto in your daily life? Is it best to keep it up or use it as a tool for one purpose? Here are some rules to help you live your Pareto life.

1. Apply the Pareto principal to many different situations. Then, choose the one that has the most positive effects. It is great fun to apply Pareto to all sorts of situations. Once you are familiar with the Pareto principle, you will see its value everywhere. In terms of time management, you might be able to come up with the idea of structuring

your private and professional lives according to the Pareto principles. The Pareto principle is a great help in your professional life. However, it doesn't work in your personal life. If you are able to do that, it is a smart thing to keep applying the Pareto principles to your professional life. It can be detrimental to apply the Pareto rule to too many situations. You may end up having to analyze each situation before being able to tackle it.

2. Pareto principle dependency should be avoided. Don't quit working on something just to make it fit into the 20 percent of activities leading to eighty% of the results. The Pareto principle can be an effective way to manage time, but in some cases it can become a dependency. Pareto basically forces you to be more productive every day. Sometimes it goes so far that people feel ashamed to do something that isn't productive. It is fine to do nothing or to spend the evening in front of a television.

Nobody forces you to adhere to the Pareto principle. Pareto principle is good for moderation. If you make too many efforts to live your daily life according to it, it could have adverse effects. Enjoy the process and you'll feel better. When you realize that the Pareto Principle ends in stress, it is time to quickly untie the knot and look objectively at your situation. Don't be afraid to admit your limitations and be truthful with yourself.

Use the Pareto Principle to become an entrepreneur

Twenty percent of customers are responsible for eighty percent the profits of many companies. This is one reason why the Pareto Principle is so appealing to entrepreneurs. It's not unusual for customers to account for 80 percent of the problems. The eighty percent of customers that make 20% of all purchases can lead to a business not being able to continue its operations. How do you structure your company according to the Pareto principle

It's important to first focus on your key customers. Many companies have both large and small customers. These large customers represent twenty percent and eighty percent respectively of a company's total profits. Because they account for a large portion of your annual income, these customers must be treated well. It is important to pay attention to these customers and ensure they are satisfied with the products or services you offer. Keep in touch with these customers to ensure they don't lose interest in you. They may switch to another company. This will make it less likely that you lose these customers.

Next, think about ways to increase your chances of attracting such customers. You should also consider the following question: Which twenty-percent of your marketing activities result in eighty per cent of the customers within your company? Do these customers make up the majority of your company's profit, or just 20%? Find out how to win more large customers and get them to continue to choose your company as their partner.

You should also consider closing down some branches of your business in the third step. Is it better to focus solely on big customers, or ignore the small streams of income? Then you can act according the answer.

The Pareto principle can be applied to your company and you will also begin to look at how you can optimize work processes. Are small changes sufficient or do you need to overhaul your entire company? Entrepreneurs must think about ways to maximize profits and save money if they are to succeed.

Pareto's principle says that twenty percent lead to 80% of the results while twenty percent lead to 80%. Many people now think that only eighty percent should be done. Although this concept works well in many cases it also has its limitations. The important thing to remember is that even the tasks that only result in 20% of the results may be vital for the company. Answering emails, for instance, isn't one of the twenty percent tasks that results in eighty per cent of the results. But, you should answer all your emails. You will miss many important messages. It can be customer questions, appointment suggestions and cooperation. The same principle applies to many tasks. If you apply the Pareto principle firmly and assume that eighty per cent of the tasks are redundant and don't need to be completed, then you might end up with nothing.

People who understand the limitations of Pareto principles and know how they can be used to improve the company's performance and grow in specific business areas are better able make changes.

Here are three additional cases where the Pareto Principle could prove to be valuable for entrepreneurs

* Customer acquisition: What twenty percent of customer acquisition strategy leads to eighty% of customers? Every business has customers. This is especially true if you are in a highly competitive market. You need to reach your potential customer before the competition. Marketing costs can be cut by knowing which strategies are most successful and which ones don't. Many ways can be used to acquire customers. There are many ways to acquire customers. However, certain methods work better than others. Pareto's principle helps you understand your expenses better and allows you only to invest in marketing strategies that are going to make up eighty percent.

* Recruitment of staff. Some companies have twenty percent of their employees responsible for eighty% of their success.

Companies will gladly accept hardworking and creative people. Employees are a key part of any company's success. Therefore, you need to really get to know your employees before you make a hiring decision. You should do some research on potential candidates before inviting them to interview. It is a good idea to hire people before you interview them. They will be the ones who make up eighty percent for your company's success.

* Problems within your own company: In most instances, 20% of all problems are caused or contributed by the employees. These could be employees, customers, partners or even customers who are causing problems. This is why you need to be able to manage such situations. You can use the Pareto Principle to help you in this situation. It teaches that such a situation should not be considered abnormal. Customers who are unhappy with your products or services will continue to be customers. But, you

don't need to shut down your business. Instead, work to avoid causing any problems. As entrepreneurs, we must anticipate that problems will occur and solve them. However, we all know that only 20% of our ideas will lead to eighty% of the solution.

* Product selection. Pareto can play a key role in product choice. Many companies have 20% of their sales coming from products. Of course, this applies only to certain companies. You will find that your distribution is accurate if there aren't many products on your shelves, such as a supermarket. However, if there are a handful of products online, it may be a small shop selling a limited number of products. The truth is that just 20% of the products are responsible for eighty percent percent of all sales. A good product is essential for any entrepreneur. You should remove any unprofitable products off your shelves and make sure you have new products for your

customers. Pareto means that every product that is not contributing to at least eighty percent should be taken out of your selection. This is a common misconception. The true calculation should be whether a product can be profitable. If it's still profitable, you should continue selling it. This is true especially for digital products such online courses, audiobooks or e-books. Sometimes products sell less than others. However, these digital products don't have the urgency to be taken offline. It is common to assume that many products are a good thing, and may even help increase revenue. But, this doesn't change the fact of the fact that 80 percent of sales are generated from 20% of the products.

* Outsourcing. Entrepreneurs should improve their time management. A successful entrepreneur will be able to focus on what is important in his company and gain an advantage over his competition. He will be able spend more time on key

projects, find new revenue streams, and explore new business opportunities. This is precisely why entrepreneurs should outsource tasks. Pareto's principle states that twenty percent is spent on your company, and eighty percent on the results. If you take on too many tasks that another person could do, you'll lose money. It is important that entrepreneurs outsource less-demanding tasks. One example is hiring a virtual assistant to answer all your emails and handle social media messages. A virtual assistant could answer your emails and handle your bookkeeping. You can also outsource entire business functions, such customer acquisition, by outsourcing them. In many cases, this will even help you save money. You'll be able to spend more time on tasks that actually move your business forward.

The Pareto principle of nature

Pareto principles can be found everywhere in nature. While the Pareto Principle is not a law in nature and does not apply to all situations, it allows for many connections to be drawn and can be used to compare and contrast. For example, twenty percent of the nations are responsible for 80 percent of environmental pollution.

Many of the traits we humans share with animals also apply, especially in areas like sexuality, herd behaviour, and more. In some cases, it has been proven that 80 per cent of animals are sired by only 20 percent of the animals. Eighty percent also see twenty percent more animals as their predators.

Pareto is also a good way to describe strong competition among animals, as it often leads to stronger ones developing while weaker ones dying. In these cases, the ratio is usually twenty-to-eighty.

The Pareto rule has no limitations. People who are trained to recognize the Pareto rule will soon be able see it everywhere. The

Pareto Principle is always present, no matter where you look.

Chapter 5: The Pareto principle's advantages and disadvantages

Advantages of Pareto's principle

There are many benefits that the Pareto principle can offer. Five advantages are offered by the Pareto Principle.

1. Focus at work: By using the Pareto rule for yourself, it is possible to be more focused because you know what tasks are important. Pareto principles are not used by everyone. However, the Pareto principle reveals that only 20% is essential and that eighty percent of the work shouldn't be given high priority. It can be postponed if there are doubts. Pareto principles also help us to organize our work. You should break down your tasks into important (not particularly important), and unimportant (very important). This allows you to assign priority to the tasks. Tasks of highest priority must be completed right away, while less important tasks can wait. If you don't have the time or desire to complete a task

quickly, they can be deferred. You can learn the Pareto principle and how to organize your thoughts so you can focus on what is important. You will soon have the same attitude in your personal and professional lives. You will work hard to achieve your goals and only take 20% of the tasks that will lead to them.

2. Discovery of your personal strengths: It is important to give up tasks you don't have the ability to do. Focusing on your strengths helps you focus more on the tasks that you can't do. Successful people are not focused on the weaknesses of their peers, but instead on their strengths. If you focus only on your weaknesses, you'll have fewer strengths at one point. Pareto principles essentially says that. You can only achieve eighty per cent of the results if you are able to do twenty percent. It is essential to know your strengths, weaknesses and how you can work towards your goals. What are you best at? What talents do not you have? You

should not be ashamed about your weaknesses. Instead, be proud and happy with your strengths. To achieve the highest performance in your chosen field, you should not only build on your weaknesses but also your strengths. The Pareto principle allows you to discover and then use your strengths. This will improve your self-confidence. It will help you recognize what tasks you can trust yourself with, and which tasks should be left to someone else. After the process is complete, recognize your strengths and it will support you for many years.

3. Do not take on unnecessary tasks. Many people believe they have to answer every email or check their social media. Sometimes you forget that you have only a few valuable tasks in your life. These are difficult to identify because you need to forget everything that has held you back the past few decades. It is often difficult for people to gauge the value and impact of a

task. They believe that every task, however small, could make a difference in their lives. This misconception is common. These are usually unnecessary tasks and do not bring about any positive changes in life. Write down all the tasks you have every day. Then, remove any unnecessary tasks or distractions. This could include social media, instant messaging, social media, people who do not suit you, and other distractions that can distract you away from your work or your goals. Be sure to get rid of the things that keep you down and from reaching your goals.

4. Rapid progress: Focusing on strategies that are quick to implement will allow you to celebrate many successes. The Pareto principle allows you to filter out tasks that will take you further. These tasks can be focused on and completed with care. You'll achieve 80 percent of your results in only twenty percent of time. This concept is also applicable to professional and personal

lives. You'll be able to reach your personal goals and make significant progress in your job. You might want to be promoted, or you may just want to raise your salary. You will quickly outperform your peers if you concentrate on the twenty percent of the work that produces eighty% of the results. It is the same with your personal goals. You'll be surprised at how quickly it is possible to achieve your personal goals if you only do the right tasks, and you do them with diligence.

5. Increases freedom: You'll have more time to do what you enjoy. With virtually every minute of work, you save time. Even if the Pareto principle was not in your vocabulary, you would still have to work towards your goal as normal. You don't have the obligation to work eighty percent, so if you are happy with your performance, you can spend more of your time with the people and things you care about. For example, you might spend more time spending with your

children and friends. You could travel, dine out, or do whatever else you desire. Pareto helps you live more fully and balances work-life.

Of course, the list doesn't end there. There are many more reasons for Pareto. This is precisely why you should have your own experiences with Pareto principles and find out if they work for you. Only after you have experienced the Pareto Principle yourself, will you understand its value.

Pareto principle's disadvantages

Pareto has its benefits, but also its disadvantages. In this chapter, we'll be looking at five of those disadvantages.

1. Ratios may be wrong. The Pareto Principle's 80/20 ratio is intuitive and easy to remember. Most of the things we remember quickly and find intuitive, we forget. This is a mistake. The eighty-to-twenty ratio is not always accurate. The Pareto principle cannot be applied to every

situation. Before you can apply the Pareto Principle, make sure you have checked the correct ratio between elements. You can't achieve eighty per cent of the results doing only twenty per cent of the work. Or perhaps your work is unique and the Pareto principles may not apply. Do not blindly trust the Pareto Principle. Instead, think through your situation and use it when it makes sense. Don't forget that the Pareto rule does not have to be an 80/20 ratio. It can, for instance, be a ninety twenty to twenty or forty-seventy ratio.

2. While many tasks may not result in many results, they are still important. The Pareto Principle assumes that you have tasks that are vital to your progress and that of the company. But it assumes that others tasks are less significant. It does not mean that all the tasks are insignificant. Let's take, for example the idea of starting a business. We know it is vital to identify a good business idea and develop a product. Then we need

to market it. This could represent twenty percent, or eighty percent, of the tasks required to achieve the desired results. There are many other tasks necessary for the continuation and growth of the business. These include writing invoices and answering emails. Although they might not be the most important tasks for your business, they are vital.

The same principle applies in other situations. Consider, for example, if you desire to become a strong athlete. You already know you need to exercise and you should eat healthy foods. It could be that twenty percent of your tasks lead to eighty per cent of the results. If you don't get enough sleeping, take enough breaks, and create a plan for training, you'll never see the results you are looking for.

Therefore, it is important that you don't ignore the 80 % of tasks that result in twenty percent of the success. They often act as the link to success. These tasks will not allow you to achieve the success you want. You should always consider which tasks of the 80 percent are really necessary for your success.

3. Quality of work may be lower: Sometimes it is possible to deliver only eighty per cent of the quality if one works only twenty percent. In certain industries, this is impossible. This is especially true if the customer expects the best. An example: A shoe manufacturer might not make shoes that are too small, simply because he can work less. The Pareto principle also has its limits. These limits are especially evident when it is about high-quality products, top services, and top performance for all types.

You could work less, produce fewer goods, and lower the prices to solve the problem. Or you could get better at what you do so you can provide the same quality service in a shorter amount of time.

You can also apply the same approach in your private life. If you put less effort into something, you might get fewer results. This is your decision. It is important to minimize the 20% of tasks that are not directly related to the results. Focus more on the tasks that yield eighty% of the results. This will enable you to live your life and work in your company with Pareto principles without having to produce lower quality.

4. Physical exhaustion. The Pareto rule can also cause physical exhaustion. Pareto is a principle that allows people to work less and creates a better work/life balance. Pareto is also seen by some as a way to have more fun and accomplish more things. This is when exhaustion can happen. You may feel exhausted from work or have a feeling of burnout. Try to find a balance between work and personal time. Pareto should never be used to make you exhaustion. Pareto principles are a time management strategy. They should help you make more

time for yourself. It should not be a cause of physical exhaustion. Avoid exhaustion by taking enough breaks and using strategies such the Pomodoro Technique while working.

5. Focus on the concept: Too many people put too much importance on the idea. The Pareto principle works in many cases, but it shouldn't be your only focus. The Pareto principle is not a fixed concept. You need to be flexible and not become too attached. Every task you do does not need to be part of a set of tasks that account for eighty percent. Pareto principles can quickly become a problem, especially when it comes to your private life. Is it better to do something for your partner and not be asked, or is it more sensible to decorate the living area? These tasks can be assigned to the twenty percent responsible for eighty per cent of the final results, or to the remaining 80 percent. People who ask such questions can apply the Pareto Principle to

too many problems. It is not necessary to rationalize every action.

Pareto's principle has its merits and its drawbacks. The benefits of the Pareto principle outweigh the cons. In most cases they will help you get more from your life and work, make it easier to manage your time more effectively and allow you to spend more of what you really enjoy.

Chapter 6: The Pareto Principle

Vilfredo Parato, an economist, said that 20% of the causes of life's events are responsible for 80%. This is the Pareto Principle. This principle can be applied to your career and interpersonal relationships to improve productivity. This chapter will cover the practical application and details of this principle.

Introduction to the Pareto Principle

Vilfredo Paraeto, economist, discovered that 20% owned 80% of Italy's lands. Further research revealed that this pattern was similar across Europe. This observation of uneven wealth distribution was the basis of Pareto's principle. This is still true today. PolitiFact says that the wealth earned by the 400 most wealthy Americans is greater than the combined wealth of all Americans. This is unlikely to change, as many of these people will still be passing their wealth on to their children and their families.

Inequality all around

Dear God was the platform where rapper Dax vented his frustrations when he said that he didn't get why some people had over 100 million dollars in their savings while others couldn't afford their daily meal. The Pareto Principle is founded on the growing inequality in our world. It is still possible to apply it to your benefit if you are able to understand its practical application. As an example, 20% of employees can be responsible for 80% of the company's profits.

Additionally, more than half the world's people are made up of individuals from a mix of countries such as the US, China, Japan and Russia. Every endeavor in life has a higher concentration. This may seem contrary to your beliefs, but it's the reality of our world. Jordan Petersen wrote 12 Rules For Life. He analyzed how life is unfair. Certain people are at the top of different endeavors because of inheritances and chance, while others struggle and fight for anything great.

His advice is to accept that reality and figure out a way to get there. If you don't, it will frustrate you and reduce your quality of life. This holds true even for the problem of racism. Racism exists in most of Europe and the USA. Yes, there should be efforts to stop this evil but victims must face it and accept that they are not immune to the consequences.

Life Is Unfair

Many people feel tempted to just let things happen. Just because it took you four decades to achieve something doesn't mean it won't happen to someone else in four months. This is the irony in life. The modern world has many machines that enable us to achieve greater results without the effort of our ancestors. Imagine the difficulties faced by early humans when trying to make fire. But, today we are "fire lords". Technological advancement has allowed us to start fires with just a few clicks of our fingers.

This is an example of how our lives are today. It is not necessary to travel by foot or horse for many weeks or months. In a matter of hours, you can reach any continent in the world today, regardless where it is located. Today's ancestors worked harder than us, but we are doing more intelligent work than they could. Although you might be able to point out some of the drawbacks of living today, the truth is we have never been more intelligent and sleek in history. Future years will bring more innovations in science, technology and engineering. Indeed, we are fortunate in many aspects to be part and parcel of the modern world.

Study of Chelsea-Bayern

The UEFA Champions League Final match between Bayern Munich & Chelsea is a good example of life's unfairness. Bayern had 43 shots on goal and 7 on target. Chelsea had nine shots on goal and only 3 on target. Bayern had 20 corner kicks to Chelsea's one. Guess what? You are correct! Chelsea scored from their one corner kick.

Bayern had scored earlier, and Chelsea scored at the last moment when all hope seemed lost. Bayern was awarded a penalty but they missed it. Chelsea won the match, winning after a penalty shootout. People praise the Chelsea side's perseverance, but this match is a prime example of how things can get out of control when there are many reasons they should be.

Working smart

There is no need to lament the unfairness of life. Instead, you should make the most of it and get the most from your life. We are wired to believe we can only achieve the best life by working hard. However, this is not always true. Working smarter than hard is better. During college, a friend called me to question how I seemed to get high grades without having to work as hard. I understood her confusion. She was hardworking and spent a lot of her time in the library, even when there were no lectures. However, her grades didn't match her efforts. Initial, she believed it was because I had more intelligence.

However, she was determined to ask me for advice on how she could get high grades like me. During our conversation, she learned that my method was what gave us an advantage. She noticed that I was not just learning, but was also more aware about the psychology of the lecturer. I would pull out every question possible from the materials and answer them, rather than trying to memorize all the information. My grades were excellent, as I spent more of my time answering the questions than reading the books. My method helped many colleagues.

You can make smart decisions about every aspect of your career, leadership, goal setting, relationships with others, marriage, and career. In the next chapters, we'll discuss how to apply this principle in order to live the fulfilled and fulfilling life you deserve. You will become more productive and happier when you recognize the areas that need your attention. This will enable you to find the most productive parts of your life so that you can reduce your investments in them. Time is a precious resource that you cannot control, and cannot afford to lose. You need to maximize your time so that you are able to focus on the most important and meaningful parts of your life.

Chapter 7: Leveraging Pareto Principles in Your Career

"Find what you love doing and get paid to do it."

Katharine Whitehorn

Prioritizing Your Area Of Concentration

Remember, the Pareto Principle revolves around finding your zone of concentration. Also, identify the most valuable aspects of your life. Then, invest your energy in these areas. These are some ways to apply this principle to your job:

Find Your Passion

Our jobs are essential to our daily lives. Pew Research Center estimates that nearly half of Americans identify themselves according to their job descriptions. The sad truth is that more than half of American employees are disengaged from their work. This is concerning. Do not accept a job that is not right for you. It is true that all jobs are stressful in one way or another. If you love your job, it can increase your chances for job satisfaction.

Katharine whitehorn's words at beginning of chapter summarize the best approach for making career decisions. Finding something you enjoy will help you maximize your talent. It will make you feel happy and enable you to give your best every morning. Emmanuel Kant vehemently condemned the tendency of treating human beings at work as machines. This is what many people have become. They don't take care of their physical and mental health. Instead, they work to earn money. These problems can be solved by discovering your passion and creating a career around it.

Prioritize Your Passion

As a college freshman, I found a group who was enthusiastic about helping each other improve academically. It was a refreshing change in my life. It allowed me to display my academic talents and helped other people improve, which is what I have always loved. This is why I wrote self-help books. At some point, however, the leader started to diverge away from the main objective. He wanted us explore extracurricular opportunities.

I think he was bored with the routine and pursuit of academic excellence. I was clear that I could no longer continue to join the group. At that point in time, academic excellence was my top priority. I would not let anything distract me. I made my painful exit from the group and set up a new one which would be focused solely on academic excellence. Many of the people I left the group joined. I was eventually asked by the leader of the group to help him with his academics. This is what you call the power of concentration. Your passion should be your top priority. Distractions can be eliminated and you must focus.

Invest in Passion

Doing well is more important than doing anything. If you're not ready to spend your time, effort, and money on a career, it's not worth it. Your job is your main source of livelihood. It provides the resources necessary to be a positive influence on others' lives. This is why you shouldn't take it for granted. Let everyone around know that you value what you do and will do your best to succeed.

Attend seminars, read books and get mentorship from people who are experts in your field. This should be done in the early stages of your life. Hindus believe in four phases of human life. They are called the Ashramas. Brahmacharya (the first phase) is the first twenty-five year of your life. It should be used to discover your passion, learn, and invest heavily in it.

Share your passions with others

In a world of different career paths and different roles, it can be easy to become intimidated. Each job is crucial to the functioning and growth of our society. How would society cope if everyone was able to become doctors or lawyers? Who would tend to the farms and supply us with food? People who give their time to caring for adults and teaching children aren't well-respected because they don't earn much.

However, it is important to be proud of your work. It doesn't matter if you don't feel proud to share your work with others. You should be able, wherever you may be, to speak up about your profession and claim to be an expert in the field.

Enjoy Your Work

Nicki Minaj wrote in a tweet early in 2020 that she had wasted three years of her life because of not enjoying the moment. Even if your dream job is a success, you may still find it difficult to be happy if every moment doesn't count. Let the happiness of every moment be your reward.

You are performing an important job. Remind yourself daily. Take pride in yourself and work hard to achieve your goals. You don't have time for negativity and negative emotions. Even during the worst times, be grateful for your job. This is the most you can do for your career in today's ultra-competitive world.

Reconsider Your Decision

It is wonderful that you find your passion and create a career from it. But it is essential to be honest and seek a new career path if your passion has waned. You can lose your meaning and frustration if you fail to do this. Arthur Brooks discusses in "From Strength to Strength" how to recognize when it is time to move to a career path that allows your crystallized intelligence to be utilized.

He explained that you have two types of intelligence: your fluid intelligence (your ability to solve complicated problems and think up new ideas) and your crystallized intellect (your ability to use knowledge and experience to solve them). Our fluid intelligence declines as we age while our crystallized Intelligence improves with time. Brooks aspired to be the greatest French Horn player of all time. It was his passion. He was dedicated to the art. He found out that his skills were diminishing, regardless of how hard he tried.

He ended up becoming a social scientist to be able to share his knowledge with the world. It's never too late if you want to change your career path and maximize your potential. This law of gravity applies to our careers. It can only go up and then drop again. Even if Lionel Messi is your favorite football player, you can't keep playing for ever. Failure to quit will cause you to lose your glory, and the criticisms will only get louder. The end of a steep curve is the beginning a new one, which will make you happy and productive if you recognize the early signs of your decline.

Chapter 8: Stress Management: The Pareto Principle

In order to stress out, you had to physically be near people. But social media has changed all that. There are more stressors today than ever before. In addition, lack of stress management may lead to physical and psychological exhaustion. This can make us more susceptible for illnesses and weaken our immune systems. This chapter will cover how the Pareto Principle can be used to manage stress.

Recognizing Your Most Significant Stressors

You can't avoid stress if you have clear goals. No pain, no gain. There is no way to be successful in your life and reach your goals without stress. But, stress must be managed well to prevent the devastating effects of poor management. In order to use the Pareto Principle, you must first identify your most severe stressors.

Stressors can come from your own actions or the schedule of others. However, it is important to recognize your stressors in order for you to take appropriate action. Your stress level can be attributed to 20% of your stressors. This could be even lower. It could also include your job, traffic and children. Pay attention to how these stressors affect your stress levels at different points.

Financial Pressure

Traffic and finances might be your top stressors for a month. Your stress level can rise to over 80% when you face financial pressures like paying rent, starting a business, or meeting rent. According to the Global Financial Literacy Excellence Center report and University Professor Economics and Accountancy, 60% Americans are stressed out about their finances. Half of Americans get anxious when discussing their finances.

This study demonstrates the profound impact of financial pressure on average American's mental health. The study also showed that 65% women feel stressed by their financial status, while 54% of men do. Researchers identified four key factors as a reason for financial pressure: high debt, low financial literacy (insufficient income), and money management issues. Researchers also discovered that financial anxiety is most common in young adults, financially dependent parents, and married persons with low incomes.

This study should give you an insight into why your finances have such a large impact on your stress levels. The study should also provide you with a solution. Here are some solutions.

* Increase your skills to improve your earning power

* Make an investment in financial literacy training materials

* Seek professional guidance regarding the management and control of your finances

* Improve your spending discipline

* Spend more time on assets and less on liabilities.

* Make sure to spend according to your budget

* Keep a shopping list handy.

Children As Stressors

The most stressful task in life is raising children. This can be seen through movies and real-life experience. Parents and guardians love children because they are full of energy. But sometimes, they can be unhappy and difficult. Parents who love their children are often anxious about their health. According to a study published in Journal of Caring Sciences (2012), 35% of American child suffer from stress-related problems. Meanwhile, unlike most adults, children lack effective stress management skills.

If they're stressed they can become cranky, which can cause tension at home. This can make it difficult for parents and guardians. Unresponsible and insensitive parents should not attempt to parent. If parents are unable to manage the rebellion of their children, then they resort to harsh means to control them like hitting them. Modern parenting requires a thoughtful and empathic approach. This goes beyond just providing for the children's needs. The majority of harmful and degrading content that is available on social media and mainstream media is being exposed to children today. You can't train your kids by watching what is happening around you.

Tom MacDonald stated that you can blame the rappers in You Can't Blame The Rappers

How many songs about Xanax/alcohol are we dumping?

How many kids will we kill "for we admit it's an issue?"

Probably stop if it was one our sons or one our daughters

We are aware that our target demographic is predominantly youth

Schoolchildren are encouraged to break the law.

Children imitate our actions and mimic what we say.

They'll go to prison because they did the things you told them was cool

He also said the following at one point during the song:

Half these artists can't even communicate, they just mumble their lyrics.

While the teens rebel against their parents, they are heard.

I suggest that you listen to the whole thing. It sums up what it is like to raise a child in today's modern world. If parents aren't careful, the impact can be catastrophic. A parent cannot be happy to see their child become a drug addict or gangster. When your children are acting out, it's normal to be tempted. Frustration is not the solution. Here are some suggestions to help:

* Be patient and take the time to get to know your children.

* Do not talk to your children when angry

* Learn to listen more to your children in order to win their trust and understand what their challenges are so that you can offer support.

* Pay attention to the influences surrounding your children

* Speak with a professional to get the advice you need.

Your job is a stressor

As we have said, stress is not something you can avoid. Your passion alone will not save you from work stress. Every occupation is not without its challenges. Every job has its challenges. You'll have to solve problems, meet demands, and that can sometimes be stressful. According to the American Institute of Stress 40% of workers view their job as very stressful. 25% of employees say that their jobs are the most stressful. The impact of your job can have a significant effect on your stress level.

75% believe that their current roles are more stressful than those of a generation before them. 29% of employees also say that they feel extremely stressed at their job. Stress management is therefore governed by the Pareto Principle. Your job may be responsible for up to 80% of the stress you experience. In order to be able to cope with your stress, you need to identify the causes and how you can reduce it. Here are some suggestions to help.

* Examine your relationship with your boss, and consider ways to improve.

* Develop positive relationships with your coworkers in the workplace.

* Take into consideration your suitability for your current job

* Explore more effective ways of carrying out your duties

* Increase your work-life harmony

Chapter 9: Leveraging the Pareto Principle for Goal Setting

You need to master goal setting. It can be the difference in a great year or an average one. Goal setting is a critical part of every success. It cannot be overemphasized. This chapter will show you how to apply the Pareto Principle for setting goals and realizing your dreams.

Setting targets that matter

Today, many people feel trapped by the influence of social media. People are often tempted to compare themselves to others, and to strive to surpass them. This will lead you to set goals that will not serve you long-term. Every step of the way, ask yourself why you are trying to reach your goal. If you don't, you'll act like someone without direction. Indecisiveness can waste your time and make it difficult to be consistent in any area.

Stay with Something

It's nothing special to brag about if you don't have a certain thing you are involved in consistently. You can be consistent when you have direction. It is also essential for the achievement of any goal. Consistency can help you find more effective ways of doing something. It can help you gain more experience while doing less. This is an advantage that experienced people have over newbies.

Your experiences will help you determine what works and which ones won't. An inexperienced person may resort to trial and errors, which can be frustrating. However, an experienced individual would have discovered the Pareto Principle on the field. He knows what you should do to provide the highest value. The experience will prove that the happiness of your boss is key to your enjoyment while working in a company. It is important to compliment your co-workers as well as clients, but it is your boss who will influence the other 20% of your company experience.

According to the American Institute of Stress (35% of American workers see their bosses as their main source of stress in their workplace), 35% of them are not happy with their job. If you have a difficult relationship with your boss, you may need to leave the job and seek a new one. Your boss is one of the most important goals you can set for yourself as an employee. In addition to the great experience you get from working, happiness with your boss will impact your chances for promotion.

Pick Your Battles Wisely

Many people make mistakes when it comes to setting goals. Their targets can be influenced by anger and revenge as well as envy. It is not healthy to lose your uniqueness among the modern-day rat race. You can be asked to participate in any plan if you don't know what you want. Even if your abilities are multi-talented, or you excel at several things, you can't be everything in this life. For example, you might have a strong voice, excel at sports, or be an academic prowess.

Rafael Nadal Case study

It is unlikely you will be able combine the roles of a top-tier musician, elite athlete, and professor. Rafael Nadal, for instance, is one of the most admired tennis players ever. He has received numerous awards and titles. But he is also a skilled runner. His football skills are exceptional and he could have achieved great success as a footballer. Miguel Angel, Miguel Angel was a great professional soccer player for both Barcelona and Spain. Because of this, he was able to provide guidance and support for his sons in the right direction.

Nadal claims that the hardest decision he had to make was between tennis and football. His father also said that he could be a great footballer. But, he could have been lost in a footballing world dominated by Lionel Messi & Cristiano Ronaldo. They would have overshadowed him like they have done to Robert Lewandowski & Zlatan Islamovic. Nadal's life teaches us that success is achieved by focusing on one thing. He wouldn't have achieved success if his focus was on tennis and football. Over 80% of his success as an individual was attributable to tennis.

Applying the Pareto Principle To Goal Setting

You have to be skilled in goal setting. You will have a better chance of reaching your goals if you use the Pareto principle in conjunction with goal setting. It is crucial that you are clear in what goals you have set and how you intend them to be achieved. Setting goals gives you the ability to focus, avoid distractions, and is a powerful combination with the Pareto Principle.

Discover your 20%

To apply the Pareto Principle in goal setting, it is important to start with the things you care about. Your passion for the game does not have to turn into a job. It can be something you do when your life is less hectic and you still enjoy the game. Nadal is still likely to play football once in a while. But it is unlikely that he has any plans to improve his football skills at the start of each year. He has set tennis goals as his 20%.

Nadal won't be able to achieve a goal of scoring twenty football goals every year as a professional tennis player. He will instead be more focused on perfecting his tennis techniques in order to score more, defeat more rivals, and improve his ranking. Take a page from this to discover your 20%. You should make sure your job and relationships with loved ones are a key part of this. This is a sign you value your priorities and are able to set targets that will improve your work productivity.

Even though your interpersonal relationships are not financially lucrative, they can be a great support system for your mental and emotional health. It should be a goal to improve your interpersonal relationships. This could be done through a variety activities that include spending time with your family and friends. You must invest 20% in your 20% to make 80% of success.

Chapter 10: Leveraging Pareto Principles in Interpersonal Relationships

Buddhists believe that the concept of self can only be a dream because each person is interconnected with others. This is far from reality. A person is an expression the history, evolution and contributions of his or her family and close friends. Our interpersonal relationships determine the quality of life. This aspect of your life is not something you can afford to neglect. This chapter will focus on how the Pareto Principle can be used to improve and sustain interpersonal relationships.

Modern World: A Loss of Empathy

Today, loneliness is one of the greatest problems in the world. Statista has found that 33% people worldwide feel lonely according to a global survey. Being alone is not the same thing as feeling lonely. All of us want to be together at times. It's important that you have it. It is a good idea to set aside time each day to reflect on your life and the circumstances. It is essential to have time alone to reflect on the current situation and to plan your future. You may feel depressed if there are people you don't want around.

It's not surprising that many feel lonely, as we are rapidly becoming machines. We look for new celebrities to join our ranks, but we are quick to reject them when they make errors or do things not fit with our values. We all make errors, celebrities included. Celebrities are just human beings. We forget that they are also human. People found it funny that Kanye West shared his mental health.

It was the same with Will Smith. When he heard his wife talk about her infidelity on TV, it led to many people laughing at him. The modern world has made life more difficult than ever. They find it entertaining and amusing that famous people struggle with certain aspects. This is their chance for them to believe that fame and fortune cannot buy happiness. It is vital that we have an emotional support network in this difficult world.

Existing in A Community

Authur B. Brooks observed Aspen trees. He discovered that they are interconnected which makes them stronger and more resilient. He explained the importance of building strong relationships to others to help us live happy and meaningful lives. It is absurd to believe we don't need anyone. Indeed, our decisions have the greatest impact on our lives. However, we are also influenced by the actions and words of others.

Lionel Messi could be considered one of football's greatest players. His success was made possible by the support of his teammates and coaches. He wouldn't have been able achieve this much without them. Pep Guardiola his coach, at that point in Barcelona, made him a false nine. He also sold older players like Ronaldinho, Samuel Eto'o and could have reduced his playing time. These moves gave Messi the chance to shine. His success in Argentina and Barcelona was made possible by the cooperation and hard work of his Argentina teammates.

He would be a liar if it wasn't for the kindness of others who have given him the opportunity to use his skills efficiently. It is absurd to suggest otherwise. We are meant to be surrounded by people who love and understand each other. When we live with people who do not understand us or are insensitive to our feelings, life becomes stressful and depressing. But it is easier to be motivated when you have supportive and loving people around you.

The Pareto Principle for Your Relationships

It is important to use the Pareto Principle when you are in relationships with people. You should identify the 20% that provide more value and invest more time and energy in these relationships. People we meet recently are often quick to call them friends, but this is a mistake. This is why people can betray their trust and abandon them. Friendships must be tested and proven. You might not be able to identify your true friends until you are in trouble.

If you can't imagine what your friends will do to you if you lose your job, or lose some of your privileges, then you are spending your time with the wrong people. It is important to strive to be independent to ensure that you are not a burden. However, it is a great gift to have support during difficult times. When you have support, it will make it easier to overcome illness or other challenges. You will never let anything get in the way of a good relationship.

Your Network Of Valuable People

It is unpleasant to have people in your life who can't offer you financial or emotional support during difficult times. There is a place for you to have such people in the life of your loved ones. It is true that you will lose friends as you get older, but you will still find your true friends. It is important to treat people well. You should not be the type of person who makes excuses for friends and family when they are in need.

You must be the friend you desire to have. Sow the seeds to make sure your friends are loyal and committed to each other. Your friend should be a reliable and trustworthy one. Be more than the 20% that you think adds the most value to your daily life. Be there for the 20% of people in your life that add the most value. People shouldn't be content to tolerate you. They should feel that you are an important human being and want to surround themselves with you. You can make yourself into such a person.

Chapter 11: Leveraging Pareto Principles In Your Marriage

Modern society is rapidly losing faith in marriage. Unfortunately, the world is witnessing a decline in marriage. But marriage can be a very satisfying and useful relationship when it works. Two people being able to love and support one another while raising their children independently and in a loving way is something that is truly beautiful. I believe in marriage. This chapter will discuss how you can make it work through the Pareto Principle.

What is Wrong with Our Marriages

Modern society is more open to transactional marriages. It is almost like people are hesitant to go in with only one leg and then abandon the other. So they quickly exit at the first sign of trouble. Researchers predict that close to 50% of US marriages will end up in divorce. 41% also end in divorce in the US after a first marriage. Second marriages are even more problematic. It is estimated that 60% of second marital relationships end in divorce. This is both shocking and sad. This is alarming.

Because of the effect it has on the children and society, this should worry us. Single parenting is not easy and is less effective than when the parents have both their children. It can be difficult for the spouse and child to move the child of another spouse into a new home. The fact that the children are not living with their parents is a negative thing that will affect their social and emotional development.

Children from broken homes are more likely to struggle with identity and lack empathy. This is because they have not been raised in an environment of love and kindness. They've seen their parents abuse their children, especially their mothers. This has a negative impact on their outlook. Many of these young people become criminals and contributes to the many vices that we have today. If homes crash at alarming rates, it is not our problem. We all are affected by this tragic pattern of life today, whether directly or indirectly.

Learning from the right models

These days, fakehoods and scripted lifestyles seem to be the norm with social media influencers. Advertisers often promote products they do not use. This is all in the name of making a profit. Unfortunately, many people who are younger today learn about romantic relationships from the wrong group of people. This is one problem in our society. Romantic relationships, especially with celebrities, are well-known today. Two celebrities sharing their feelings for "eachother" is a romantic sight that everyone loves. These stunts usually don't end well.

It's full a show and pretense. Many of them will break up after entertaining their friends.

Sometimes, the love affair may lead to pregnancy and birth of children. This is dangerous because we are used to having "baby mommas" as the norm. Yes, marriage requires a lot of commitment. But it's worth it if it's the right person. Unfortunately, some people's judgments have been clouded by their desire to marry a famous couple.

They have destroyed every other virtue that is essential to their marriage, including patience, empathy, resilience, perseverance, and endurance. This way of thinking is not sustainable and is damaging our society. It is time we celebrated couples who have been married for at least twenty-three, thirty, or even forty years. It's possible if we know our priorities. Marriage should not only be a matter of convenience. They should work together to create a better future for their children.

The Pareto Effect on Your Wedding

We can have strong and fun marriages by using the Pareto Principle. Many marriages fail because of "irreconcilable conflicts." Although people change, there is no irreconcilable conflict if the spouses want to make the marriage work. A person once asked me what I consider the most important element that makes a marriage succeed. I said that the couple must refuse to quit their marriage (as well, mutual respect which is often lacking).

It doesn't matter if the couple is willing to continue the marriage, and have mutual respect for each other, it won't end. Unfortunately, today's generation is not willing to persevere and have patience in order to make things work. If there is a problem, people are ready to find a solution. This attitude shows in our political approach, how we support a soccer club, and also in our relationships. If you're not yet married, it is a sign that you have many ex partners. If you struggle to keep close friends, it could be a sign that you might have trouble maintaining a marriage.

You can determine if you have an attitude of incontinence by how you treat your friends. The way you treat friends can tell you how your tolerance, patience and loyalty levels. There is no way to transform yourself into a different person after the ceremony. You need to be intentional about improving your self-esteem. It is a false assumption to assume your spouse will treat your partner better than your friends. Over time, all the butterflies in your belly will end up natural dying. It is your relationship with your spouse and the quality of that friendship that will be rediscovered.

Finding the 20% in your Marriage

Understanding your partner is crucial to maintain a positive environment in your marriage. Women and men are different. It is a huge mistake to compare your spouse with someone else. It hurts when others compare you with other people. You shouldn't do the same thing to your spouse. It is best to learn the love language of your spouse. You might not be able to give your spouse expensive gifts. Perhaps your spouse would prefer you cook at the home and have fun doing it.

You won't get the same pleasure from taking her to a restaurant. Your spouse shouldn't be forced to do what you want. The 20% that matter most to the person you are marrying will determine 80% your happiness. You should discover these things and be more interested in them than trying to satisfy everyone else. A relationship is only successful if there is a willingness to compromise. It is important to allow your partner to have their way sometimes as long as it does no harm to your core values.

Chapter 12: Leveraging Pareto's Principle of Leadership

According to career satisfaction statistics the most productive employees show a willingness to come to work every day with the goal to solve problems, meet specific targets and weather the storms. This is something every leader strives for, but it is difficult to achieve. This chapter will explain how the Pareto Principle can help you achieve your best leadership results in any role.

Leadership Is Key

"Everything rises or falls on leadership."

John C. Maxwell

Leadership plays an important role in the success or failure of any institution or organization. The team's strategy and goals are set by the leader. A leader is responsible for setting the goal and developing a plan to achieve it. Red, the animated bird movie Angry Bird 2, wanted to lead a group of birds-pigs against the eagles. Red was passionate about the cause and had great intentions, but the other members of the team saw that he had no idea or plan on how to achieve his goal. You should remember that leadership is more than just leading an organisation. As a parent you are the leader of your children. The husband is supposed to be the leader of his wife's children.

The Pareto Principle can be applied to any capacity. The Pareto Principle can be used to help you lead. You need to identify your key team members as well as the most productive activities within your team. Once you identify the most committed members of your team, then they should be your primary focus. It is a wasteful of time to put effort and time into people that don't desire to grow and follow the same path as your team. This is a better way to get rid of people who are not willing to grow and move in the same direction as you.

Following the Pareto Principle

People will follow you unless they believe in you and trust you. You will lose their faith in your leadership abilities if they don't see you are capable of achieving results. The Pareto Principle may be a useful tool in this regard. Here are some of the many ways you can leverage the Pareto Principle in your role as a leader

Identify the Most Successful Team Members

In the workplace, people may not be motivated the same. Some people only care about the financial gains associated with a task while others see the workplace in terms of solving problems and providing value. While such people need to be paid, they are willing to do the extra work to make sure the team meets its goals. While leaders wish to have such people, the truth is that they are not common. They are not difficult to find however.

You can be a leader by knowing how to put more emphasis on the best members of your team and not reject the others. It will cause discord if you reveal your favorite team members. This is vital in parenting. You should not tell your kids that you have a favorite kid. It can lead your children to make unhealthy comparisons that could cause a break down of the family. It is a shameful thing to be the cause of your children's hatred.

Avoid Sentiments

When you reward those who do not show similar commitment and loyalty, it will send the wrong signal to your loyal followers. My mentor once advised me that rewarding people who aren't loyal to you is going to discourage your loyal followers. This sentiment is usually due in part to the abilities of these people. All of us want people with the skills to do certain tasks efficiently. However, loyalty should not be sacrificed for talent. It's much easier to find talented individuals than it is to find loyal employees.

You will find loyal, committed people who are willing to invest in you. Your duty is to educate them and help them grow. If they feel that they owe you something, it increases their loyalty. It is not necessary for everyone to own their business. It's more productive and satisfying to work alongside people who aren't treating you like a machine, and will allow you to reach your full potential. To be the leader that inspires people to solve problems and grow, you must first do this.

Keep the Door Open

It's frustrating to have people respond and cooperate less than expected. You should have the tools to punish rebellion and ineptitude, and you must be consistent. You must punish the team member responsible for an action and any team member that is not complying with your orders must also be punished. When you don't follow through, you open the door for others to doubt or rebel against your leadership. Be consistent in rewarding good behavior.

While it is recommended to punish defaulters and offenders, it is not recommended that anyone be shut out. This means that a defaulter who is ready to make amends and do better should be allowed to go back to his or her original steps. This is vital in parenting. A person's inability to complete a task or their failure to do so does not automatically mean they will never be able make amends. One way to build trust with your followers is to give them the chance for atonement. Reunions can often be beautiful. It causes the offender to want to make sure that the same thing does not happen again.

Make the Right Example

Leadership should not require coercion. Leadership should not be coercive. It is hypocritical if you tell people to do things they don't. This approach will result in you losing the respect of your followers. Your followers will protest you if they see you as a leader who is fond of breaking team rules. They will grumble when they are instructed and won't follow your commands.

If you don't set an example and lead by example, you might end up coercing or threatening them. Your followers will be more willing to follow you if you show them the values you hold dear. To be a leader you must live the vision. This is not an easy task, but it's a necessary part of leading people.

Chapter 13: Leveraging the Pareto Principle To Find Meaning and Happiness

Happiness is not impossible, despite the many unhappy people around the world. It's either that we seek it wrongly or that we don't want it. But, in the end, our greatest achievements will be the fulfillment that comes from leading a fulfilling and fulfilled life. This chapter will show you how to apply the Pareto Principle for happiness and meaning.

Happiness or Success

Brooks shares his story with a successful businesswoman. She shared her struggle with happiness, fulfillment, and success despite having achieved great success. She was at a place in her career that was declining, but she did not want it to end. Brooks asked Brooks what she needed for happiness. Brooks replied that she preferred feeling important over being happy. This is the mind state of many people all over the globe today, even though it sounds strange.

Chase Success Sensibly and Responsibly

Motivational speakers often tell us to chase your dreams, but never warn us that success is addictive. They do not tell us that success will decrease or that we will lose the fame and recognition we enjoyed at one point in our lives. Many famous and successful people are now depressed. Some people commit suicide when they are at their highest. One example is Antony Bourdain, chef. In an interview with The New Yorker, he boasted that he has the best job in all of the world. He was a well-known celebrity who took part on two TV shows, Parts Unknown as No Reservations.

The unimaginable did occur on June 8, 2018. Famous French chef, he hanged his self in a hotel in France. It was later discovered that he was having problems with his partner and was struggling with alcohol addiction. He was a workaholic, which could have contributed further to the problems. Someone who works so hard and doesn't make time for his family will experience loneliness. He will also have a hole in his life that is impossible to fill.

You don't have to choose between happiness, success or both. Problem is, many people will risk their health and families to become celebrities. They want to be in the spotlight and get noticed. Your career should be your best but it doesn't have be at the expense your mental health and your relationships.

Happiness: The Pareto Principle Formula

According to Harvard Study of Adult Development, our happiness is directly related to how we relate to others. We would be foolish not to give importance to this aspect of life. This shows that 80% of our happiness can be attributed to the relationship aspect. The truth is that life can seem unfair and difficult. How do you explain Ludwig van Beethoven's profound deafness as he began to blossom into a world-class performer? He was able to overcome the difficulties and find a way to display his talents.

Stressful and sad events can happen in life. You can weather any storm by having a strong network who cares about and supporting you. Authur B. Brooks described investing in your relationships with others as "cultivating the Aspen grove". This is key to your happiness. This has been proven by both research and observation. But, many people will choose to spend more time with fantasy things that offer little or no lasting satisfaction. For example, social media and digital devices.).

At first, I thought it was a great way for me to relax. When I spend more time with it, however, it can negatively impact my feelings of relaxation. Your internet surfing habits can be affected by your visits to social media pages. Because of their social media addiction, many people experience the Fear Of Missing out (FOMO). FOMO can be described as anxiety caused by the feeling that they are missing out of new experiences through social media.

Do What Makes you Happy

A typical day will have many activities. You might like to meditate, cook, pray or visit a friend. The majority of things we do during a day are important. These are essential to maintain our pace in life. They don't always play an important role in our happiness. For example, cooking is healthy and a way to save money. But, I don't like to cook.

It makes me feel stressed and takes away from other activities. I'm sure there are others with a different opinion. Some of my friends love to cook and are content when they do so for others. Although they love receiving compliments about their meals from others, that doesn't appeal me. To understand yourself and find the 20% of things that are important for your happiness, you need to be authentic. Being able to converse with intelligent people who are intellectually and spiritually minded makes me feel alive.

It's something I love doing. I can eat without thinking for hours if I am having an intellectual and meaningful conversation with someone who is on the exact same page. Sports is also a good option. It is highly recommended that you find your passion and spend more of your time doing it. The time in life is too precious to be under immense pressure. Being responsible is a sign you do the right thing. However, relaxation and pleasure should not be denied. Take a moment for yourself and relax. It is a gift that you are able to give yourself.

Chapter 14: Summary of the root cause of all our problems

Lifestyle-related causes of daily problems

Poor lifestyle choices, unhealthy lifestyles and bad habits are all factors that can lead to so many personal problems. Negative lifestyle choices can lead directly to various social, mental, and physical problems.

Here's a list highlighting common lifestyle-related issues that cause everyday problems.

* Poor exercise habits

* Addiction drugs

* A lack of sleep

* Excessive rest

* A sedentary existence

* Eating disorders

* Chronic diseases

All day problems are often caused by the human factor

The chances of you experiencing anxiety, mood swings or depression are high.

Here are some examples for human-factor causes of everyday issues:

* Poor listening skills

* Ego Threats (criticism).

* Poor self-image

* Feelings a lack of worthiness

* Lack of understanding

* Fearful attachment towards results

* Interfering relations

* Inadequate feedback

* Social rejection

* Relationship conflict

* Selfishness

* Workplace politics

* Inadequate boundaries

* Inflexible Thinking

* Insecure attachments

* Lack of self discipline

* Inadequate life skills

* Not doing your best

* Taking things personally

Administrative causes of everyday problems

It's possible that your problems at work, your business, or your productivity are due to administrative issues.

Here are some examples:

* Lack of improvement/stagnation in a skill that you care about

* Inadequate planning and resources are required to execute the plan

* Having the wrong priorities. Overly focusing attention on irrelevant things. Not enough focusing upon things that matter.

* A goal you set that is too ambitious and not in line with your abilities.

* Setting a small goal that doesn't motivate you enough is not going to bring you success.

* Inadequate Feedback on any of the above (or other) to gain an understanding about what's working.

* Bad execution - putting into action.

These three categories are not an exhaustive list of root causes for everyday problems. There are many other root reasons for everyday problems.

Chapter 15: Theory of the Root Causes for Everyday Problems

Problem-solving techniques that make it easier to find the root of the problem faster.

An outline

Step 1 Identify the problem. Step 1: Identify the problem. What are the consequences of the problem.

* The Apparent problem

* Define your problem

* What Are the Reasons for the Problem

* Root Cause Identification

Step 2 Analyze and solve the problem. Step 2 Analyze the problem. Causes of the problem.

* The List of Symptoms and Signs of Problem

* Possible Root Causes (List).

o The 5 Whys

Pareto rule/principle

Step 3 - Solve the problem. Solution: What can be done?

* Actual Root Cause

* Design a Solution

* Implement the solution

* Evaluate The Results

In detail:

Step 1 - Identifying the problem

Identify the problem that you must solve immediately. If the problem continues to reoccur, break it into smaller problems and tackle each one separately. As best as you can, write down what the problem is. What are my current thoughts (cognitions) as well as the physical sensations related to this issue? What is the primary problem? Can I describe it in more detail?

What are the possible causes? Why is this problem happening now? What are the contributing elements to this problem List as many contributing factors as possible.

Root cause identification

You may be having the same problem. What do you think is the root cause?

Step 2 - Analyze the problem

Once you have defined your problems, the next step in analysing them is to use these questions:

* What's the problem?

* Determine whether it is caused by an external or internal factor.

* How did this happen?

* What's the story behind this issue?

* What are the current impacts on my daily life?

* What are the solutions I have tried in the past and what were their outcomes?

* Can I find alternative solutions?

* Are there other root causes that could be causing this problem?

Take a moment to answer each question. This exercise is designed to help you gain new perspectives on how to solve everyday issues. Take as much time as you need to write.

Possible root causes

Now you will need to identify the root causes of your problem.

These can be achieved using the five whys' or Pareto principle' techniques.

The five whys

"The Five Whys" method systematically asks why five times to reach the core of a matter.

Consider this: A person who procrastinates might think about asking themselves these questions:

Why did I decide to finish this project? Because I want the opportunity to make money.

Why do I want money? Because I need to eat.

Why am I required to purchase food? Because without food, my body becomes weak and eventually dies.

Why do I need food and water? Because I have one.

Why is it important to live? Because life's awesome!

This last answer might seem quite simple but it serves to emphasize the fact procrastination may lead to death. It will be an eye-opening revelation to some.

By breaking down a problem into smaller pieces, the five Whys can help you pinpoint the root cause.

The pareto principle

Vilfredo Paraeto, an Italian economist discovered that 80% are produced by 20% of causes.

Pareto principle may also be applied to everyday problem analysis.

If you have ten issues and analyse their causes, then eight problems could be related to just two root cause.

This principle is important as it means your goal is not to eliminate all your problems, but rather to identify and eliminate those that are most influential in the generation of the smaller ones.

This is how you can apply the Pareto rule for everyday problems analysis:

List all of the problems you would like to solve. Next, rate each one on how it affects you. You need to be honest with yourself about what you are going through.

You can divide each item into 4 categories.

* major problems (e.g.

* minor problems, e.g. "I get upset when my family disagrees publicly with me"

* Minor problems (e.g. ").

* small problems (e.g., I notice a spot on my ceiling every time I wake-up).

Each problem should be rated on a scale 1-10, depending upon how much it bothers you. The items with the highest scores are the ones you should concentrate on.

Finally, identify and resolve the problems with high ratings. This should be done objectively to ensure it doesn't become an additional problem.

Problem symptoms

Problem-solving requires that you can distinguish between symptoms and problems.

Symptoms are symptoms that result from a problem. But the root cause is what causes these negative effects.

Malignant tumours can be a sign that you have cancer, but they are not the cause.

Because it is easy to get distracted by small symptoms, you could end up ignoring the real problem. Instead of trying to solve the root cause of symptoms, my goal is to make them disappear. If someone is unable to heal an infected wound, and keeps applying bandages over it.

Once you have determined the root causes of your symptoms, it's time to create a list.

Here are some areas that you might be interested in analyzing: emotions and habits and triggers; thoughts, attitudes & belief;

physical responses (e.g.. tiredness); relationships, actions (e.g.. procrastination).

These are some common signs of everyday problems:

* Emotions - Anxiety and Fear.

* Habits and Addictions: Alcohol and drug abuse, smoking, overeating.

* Thoughts about regretting the past or worrying about the future

* Actions - procrastination, disengagement from your life

* Physical Effects: Tiredness/lack sleep, illness weight gain or loss

Once you've identified the root causes and created a list, you can see patterns in your behavior. One example is stress leading to anger and depression which then leads to procrastination. This is because there is a recurring pattern that allows problems to build up over time without ever being addressed.

Understanding the causes of everyday problems and how they can affect your behaviour is vital.

Step 3 - Solving the problem

The next step is:

* Look for possible solutions

No matter how silly they might seem, think of possible solutions. These solutions could include fixing physiological issues, removing or altering other contributing factors to your environment.

* Design a problem-solving solution

Make an action plan that outlines what you are going to do to solve everyday problems. This is your ultimate goal. You want to solve your problems right now and prevent them from happening again.

Also, it is a good idea if you include evidence that these solutions have worked in the past. You might think, "If I have too many tasks at work, I may try to leave work earlier so that everything can be completed before it's too bad." If this happens, my stress levels could rise, and I might start drinking to relax.

It should be something you will do daily for the next six month, particularly if it is a long-standing problem that has not been solved before. Even though it may seem daunting at the beginning, this will not be the end of your daily problems.

* Compare the results

Your first step is to keep following the action plan you made for at least a week. You will then need to review your progress every week and assess whether you are making progress towards solving your problem.

Chapter 16: Let's talk strategies

Let's talk strategies in solving everyday problems.

It is better to solve one problem and not have to deal with it multiple time.

Here are some ways to make everyday problems a learning experience, and increase your understanding of the reasons why they happen.

* Make a list with the top ten issues in your life. Then, identify why they happen. It's possible to add other areas of concern that you want addressed.

For each one:

* Indicate how many years you believe this problem has existed. You can create a chain linking the events in the sequence to the final problem that must be overcome to find a permanent resolution. This might involve asking yourself "why" questions as far back as you can, in order to eventually reach the

original root causes of your current problems and goals.

* This type of question will enable you to visualise your problem areas as a series of events. These are usually significant factors in your daily problems.

Let's take, for instance:

A headache is a common symptom. It is the fifth most frequently experienced condition globally. This has been made more common by overwork and poor lifestyle choices (such as smoking or drinking) in recent years.

* Some of the effects of a headache could be:

* Reduced productivity, tiredness and exhaustion at work

* Anxiety and stress in social situations, such as with friends or relatives; Depression because of the feeling that it evokes; Feeling like you're a burden to loved ones; Loss of focus and concentration at work.

* The primary cause of these problems is stress, overwork, poor lifestyle choices.

The secondary factors are individuals' reactions to each of the following:

* Exhaustion, fatigue, and decreased productivity at the workplace: Evidence suggests that it is caused by different people experiencing the problem in a different way, making it difficult for them to be fixed.

* Anxiety and stress in social situations: This problem will be more difficult to solve as there are more commonalities. These solutions will be easier to spot than those that are for tiredness/exhaustion at the workplace.

* It can be hard to see how many changes you're experiencing at work, with friends, or with loved ones. When you have enough data on each of these events, you can see the chain and make more concrete and impactful solutions. It will help identify the problem areas that you can solve on your

own and those that need to be addressed by family members or friends.

* Conduct a root-cause analysis of your problem and help others to solve theirs. Understanding the causes of your problems will help you to understand how they are solved. This will enable you to determine the right solution for each problem and help you grow personally and professionally. It will also strengthen your relationships.

Chapter 17: Feelings of fear

Fear can be defined as any negative emotion caused or triggered by an imagined or real threat to harm. Fear is when we see something as frightening.

Fear is a useful emotion that is natural and can help us in many ways. It helps us get away from danger, or to prevent it.

It prepares you for "fight-or flee" situations and helps you to avoid similar dangers later.

Fear is dangerous because we perceive things as being "dangerous," when they really aren't.

It is possible to identify and understand our fears so that we can identify areas that are holding us back. We can also stop it from controlling you.

Fear is a significant barrier to unlocking our potential. Fear keeps us from doing things we might not normally do. It prevents us solving problems and reaching our goals.

Worst of all, fear makes us feel terrible about ourselves. If fear is allowed to rule our lives, it will keep us from reaching our goals.

Fear can be a significant obstacle in our path to success and happiness. To overcome this, we need to use every ounce of strength that we have.

Here are some reasons to conquer fear

Fear is in your thoughts

* The reality lies in your actions. Fear is a mental construct. It is not real. It's possible to feel scared even if there isn't something to be afraid. Fear isn't a real thing that can make us feel like a monstrous monster. It is simply a thought in our mind that can be changed and manipulated. Fear is not something we need to control. We have the power to decide how we view things and feel about them.

Fear limits your potential.

* We all have the potential of doing amazing things in our lives. But fear often stops us from doing them.

* Fear can hold us back from our true potential. People who are successful and happy do not allow fear to stop them from achieving their goals. This is because they know they have the power to make whatever reality they want regardless of what circumstances. Fear can prevent us from taking risks and keeps us in our comfort areas. To realize our true potential, we need to fight fear with all that we have.

Fear cannot be ignored

* Fear is a significant obstacle to happiness and success. We must face it head-on. It is impossible to avoid fear by distracting yourself and pretending that it does not exist. Fear will always be there. To be freed from fear's grip, we have to face it and admit that it is only thoughts in our heads. You can live your life without regrets. Do

you let fear keep you from taking chances or achieving your goals? Then what is your life worth?

Fear dissipates your energy

* Your body is flooded with stress hormones such adrenaline when you're fearful. These hormones are there to protect you, but they can also drain your energy.

* It is possible to feel tired and irritable after feeling too afraid. This fatigue can lead eventually to anxiety or depression.

Fear causes paralysis

* Fear is a paralyzing force that prevents us taking action.

* If your fear of rejection is a problem, you might close yourself off in your own home and stay there. It is much easier to hide than to confront the outside world. This will make it difficult to do all the things necessary for life, such as connecting with people or going to work. Afraidness will

make it difficult to take advantage of many opportunities.

Fear leads to procrastination

* In times of fear, we may be hesitant to begin or complete tasks as we don't believe we can do them. Fear can cause self-doubt and encourage fear. You can defer taking action for so many days that 'tomorrow' becomes every day. Then you feel no motivation to get back to the task at-hand.

Fear is a cause of confusion

* Your mind can become clouded by fear when you're afraid. You may find it difficult to make decisions or think clearly. You might have difficulty making decisions or thinking clearly. Fear leads to doubt and hesitation, which make it hard to make good decisions about your life.

Fear makes you weak.

* You become less motivated when you feel afraid.

* It's difficult to get the energy needed to do tasks when you are overwhelmed by fear. Because of the constant flow of stress hormones through our bodies, we feel tired and drained. If this happens too often, it can quickly diminish our motivation to achieve our goals. In the end, we may never have the ability to succeed in your life.

Fear makes you irrational

* Fear makes it difficult to control our emotions. If we feel scared, our emotions are heightened and cloud reasoning.

Fear can cause a decline in our ability for rational thought. You need to be able and able to look beyond your emotions to see the big picture. It's often that you will find there is nothing to fear because it was just a circumstance or thought in the mind, not reality.

Fear makes you act like a victim

* If we feel afraid, we tend to blame external factors for our problems instead of taking responsibility. Feeling like victims can make us feel weaker and give away our power to the external world or other people. If we lose our ability to choose how we respond, it makes it more difficult for us change our lives. We don't realize that we have the power to eliminate fear from our lives.

Fear is a sign that there is an issue

Fear is a sign of something that needs to change. For instance, fear of failing at something could be a sign that something is wrong in your life. If you fear failing, you might have something in your life you are content with and don't want it to change.

The best solution to fear would be for the person feeling it, regardless of its form, to get to the bottom of it and find out how to deal with it.

The root causes behind fear

Fear of the unknown is one of its root causes. If you think about what might happen in future, you feel anxious. This causes us to feel insecure and vulnerable because we don't know what to do with things that are unknown or unpredicted. Then, our egos take over and make these fears worse by thinking "What if??" Or "What happens next?" or "What if my friends laugh at me?". Instead of focusing on what can go wrong, we dwell on what is possible and not on what can be done to make it better.

Other root causes for fear

* Uncertainty

* There is no control

* Judgment from Others

* Failure

* Uncertainty

* Self-doubt

* Vulnerability

How to eliminate fear from life

It is important to stop being afraid of the future. Everything else is susceptible to changing and shifting. No matter what you do or how hard it is, we don't know what the future will bring. Stop worrying about the future. This does not mean that you can ignore your responsibilities. Rather than allowing fear and worry to paralyze, embrace each moment without trying to predict the future.

Living in harmony with uncertainty is possible

Because we don't have a lot of knowledge about them, we can feel scared. This is normal and natural. But if you want your future to be bright, you must learn how to deal with uncertainty in healthy ways.

Sometimes we can't predict the outcome of events or external circumstances. It's futile to be worried about something we can't control. Focus on what you can control, and don't worry about what the future holds.

Let's look at ten proven ways to end fear

Face your fear head-on

It is important to face your fears straight away if you want to get rid of them. This means that you have to face your fears and get out there. If you refuse to confront what you fear, fear can't be overcome.

Exposure therapy may be a good option.

Exposure therapy helps people with fear confront their fears. The treatment involves gradually exposing them, one by one, to their deepest anxieties. The same principle applies for other types of fear. Call someone you admire, but don't really know well, and ask them for a raise.

Summary: Feel the fear, and then do it anyway.

Visualize the worst thing that could happen

Visualize the worst that could happen and ask yourself, What if it happens?

Succession is a mental technique that people use when they are afraid. They imagine the worst outcome and then consider what happens if that does not happen. This allows them to gain a better understanding and reduce their anxiety.

Then, they begin to imagine how things might turn out if the worst were to happen.

Consider this: If you have failed an exam, might you ask yourself:

"What could be the worst thing to happen? I will need to take the course again next semester. This is a manageable situation, even though it is not ideal. I can deal with it. Next semester will go better.

Avoid dwelling on the worst possible scenario. It might never happen. Instead, shift your thinking from fear to positive thoughts of how you would handle things if they did. This will ensure that you are prepared for any eventuality and have a plan of action in place to address it.

Take a look at what you could do right.

It is possible to think positively using the same method. This means that we must look at the upside of any fear or anxiety we have about something. This will enable us to change our mindset from fearful to optimistic and happy, which will help us remain motivated to achieve our goals.

Reward yourself

It is important to reward yourself for facing your fears if you want to conquer fear. When you face your fear, you could award yourself a gold star on your calendar or a pat for the job. This will motivate you to face your fears every day and will help you learn how to cope with uncertainty.

Share your fears

Fear of failing is often kept hidden, making it harder to address the problem or overcome it. Talking with trusted people who don't judge us about our fears can help us get rid off that fear. This helps us break down the walls (negative self-talk), and allows us to think of more constructive ways to handle them.

Talking about fears makes you accountable. People will be more likely to encourage you than just letting you sit there all day.

Keep your focus on your breathing

Fear can often lead to tight muscles and shallow breathing. Mindfulness is a technique that allows you to calm your mind and relax your body. This is easily achieved by focusing your attention on something in the room right now, or counting down from 10, while inhaling slowly through your noses.

Meditation is another relaxation technique. Meditation helps calm the mind and keeps you calm. This allows you to see more clearly than being distracted by anxiety or panic. Meditation has many benefits including enhanced mental, physical, emotional, and spiritual well-being; addiction relief and stress reduction; increased creativity and intelligence; improved concentration and memory; and improved focus.

Get active before you face your fears

Make sure you practice lightly before you confront your fears. It will help you feel more calm and relaxed than when you are pumped with adrenaline. This will make it easier to think clearly. Exercise can make you feel great about yourself, which can reduce your fear and nervousness.

Nature's healing power can be used to your advantage

Nature is therapeutic. It can make us happy and relaxed to see a waterfall or forest. This is why parks are well-known for being a good place to relax. Nature is an effective tool in anxiety disorder treatment. You can achieve this by taking a walk in a park or simply looking at photographs of nature within your home. It doesn't matter how you do this, it just matters that you harness nature's power to calm your nerves when you feel anxious.

Learn as much about your fear as possible

It is much easier to overcome fear of the unknown then of identifiable characteristics. To overcome fear of the unknown, it is a good idea for your brain to study small amounts about what you are afraid of. This will allow your brain to recognize that these fears are not frightening but unfamiliar. The best way to approach the subject you are afraid of is from a different angle. It can make it more positive.

It is possible to gain knowledge about your fear so that you can recognize it when it occurs and then take the necessary steps in order to overcome it.

Make your imagination work for you

Although it sounds strange, visualizations of yourself conquering fear can help to overcome it in real-life. People suffering from anxiety or panic disorder often use this method.

Focusing on the solution or overcoming the fear is key to making it work. Not pretending to be fearless, but using your imagination differently to help your brain prepare for real life. Imagine you are nervous about speaking in front crowds. Now imagine you doing that. Your breathing techniques will help you calm down and feel confident. This will allow your brain and neural pathways to be more familiar with the idea.

Think differently

Sometimes we must make unexpected connections in order to solve a problem that is too complex or too large for us. It's a smart idea to think outside the box when solving everyday problems. Reframe your perspectives

Sometimes, you only need to see the situation from a different perspective in order to see it differently and find solutions. Your brain has the ability to link things in special ways. This allows you to see the problem from a new perspective and solve it. This is what happens when you see a problem from a completely different perspective. Your mind connects the dots differently.

Humour can be an effective stress reliever. Humour, even dark humour has been shown to be effective in relieving stress. You can see the funny side of a problem, no matter how serious it may seem. This will help you feel happier overall.

Use mindfulness exercises

Mindfulness exercises will help you regain control and actively manage thoughts so that you don't let them control you. It is important to realize that you can control the thoughts and actions in your head, although it can be difficult. There are many reasons that we feel out of our control. However, mindfulness exercises are a great way for our brain to recognize the power we have over how our mental experience. In the subsection 'focus on your breath', I already listed two mindfulness exercises. These are meditation, and breathing exercises. These are both very helpful. Like meditation, yoga is an excellent way to bring your mind into a state of calm and allow you to concentrate on what is happening right now.

Case Study: The Fear of Water

This case studies focuses on Teri's fear of the water.

Teri has suffered nightmares of drowning since she was very young. She would often wake up screaming and ask her parents to let her sleep in their bed. She noticed the problem more when she was in high school. Teri stopped going to social events where there was water.

Teri had severe panic attacks whenever she was in close proximity to water. She suffered from crying spells, fast breathing, extreme sweating and panic attacks.

Teri was eventually referred by her doctor to receive aqua therapy at a local hospital. The therapy consisted of Teri being immersed into the water and then slowly increasing her time floating by herself.

Teri's first sessions of aquatherapy were set up so that Teri was not alone in the pool. Gradually, Teri was able to float by herself for longer periods of her therapy sessions.

Teri's fear began dissipating after several sessions. She realized that the fear was something she needed to overcome and bought her own floatation device.

Gradually she increased the time she spent in water. Finally, she decided that she would go into the ocean. This was her worst fear.

Teri's tale is an excellent example of exposure therapy and how it can work. It also shows the importance for a gradual increase of intensity and time in dealing with uncommon fears.

Teri overcame her fear of water with these words:

* Her acceptance of the fact she had a problem.

* Her willingness for help.

* Her ability take small steps to expose her body; her body can relax gradually.

* Understanding that she would not die in the event of an accident and that there were always options to return home and revert.

Chapter 18: Feelings anxiety

Anxiety, one of the most common mental disorders worldwide, is also a major problem. Anxiety has been described as "the most common mental illness" in the world. It's often caused by tension, worry, fear, or anxiety.

Anxiety disorders can manifest as anxiety attacks, panic attacks and worry. For people who have not experienced anxiety themselves, it can be difficult to grasp what it feels like. Some helpful analogies might help: high blood pressure with no physical manifestations, constant pins and needles because you are waiting for something terrible to happen at any given moment, living life feeling like your heart is trapped in your throat. Anxiety affects all ages and backgrounds.

These are the reasons to get rid anxiety

It reduces your chances of achieving your goals if you feel anxious. It can be difficult to concentrate when you are experiencing negative emotions such sadness, anger, and other feelings.

Interferes when you are unable to relate. Anxiety can make it difficult to bond with people as your mind is filled by negative emotions instead of positive. You can't relax enough to make lasting relationships if you feel anxious.

It causes poor health and exhaustion. Negative thoughts can cause brain fog which can lead to poor health. The mind and body are linked in a way where what one feels affects the other. Your mind can become overwhelmed by daily stressors such as work, school, or family obligations.

* It can cause emotions such as sadness and depressing that can lead to stress-related problems in your life or business.

Anxiety can be a sign that there is an issue.

Anxiety can best be understood when it's seen as a sign or symptom that you need to address in order to feel better about your life and make your life more enjoyable. Anxiety can stem from many sources, including mental and physical disorders. In some cases, anxiety may be your body's way of telling you something isn't right in a certain area of life. It is important to determine what is causing anxiety and how you can fix it.

Why are you anxious?

Anxiety can come from many sources. Some triggers are internal and others external. External factors include stress at work and home, environmental problems, traumas from the past, and other factors. The internal factors include our attitude, which can be either positive and negative, as well as our perception of reality.), and your overall mental/emotional state.

The physiological symptoms are the same regardless of how you feel it: racing heart, sweating or blank mind (where your mind is completely unresponsive to any senses of uneasiness), tightness in chest, shortness and breath...etc.

Panic Attacks, anxiety and their relationship to panic

Panic attacks aren't a mental disorder. But they can be very common in anxiety sufferers. You are more likely to experience one or several panic attacks if your anxiety disorder is present.

A panic attack can be described as a sudden, overwhelming fearful feeling. There is no known cause for panic attacks and they can sometimes be unpredicted in their severity. It is a common feeling that people experience when they feel overwhelmed.

Panic attacks could cause rapid breathing and shaking of the body.

Root causes of anxiety

1. Stress

Cortisol is a stress hormone that is produced by the adrenal glands. It can affect many parts of your body like digestion, moods as well memory retention and immune system functioning. This can lead to muscle tension and increased blood pressure. It can also make it more difficult for you sleep. These effects can lead, in particular, to anxiety disorders.

2. Depression

People who feel depressed can feel lonely and isolated from the people in their lives. This can lead them to feeling alone, or like no one is listening or caring about them. This can be a very difficult existence, causing sadness, loss, and even pain if it isn't treated with the right therapy. The likelihood of suffering from anxiety is higher.

3. Disconnection

You may feel anxious about your day. It is possible that you are disconnected from your own thoughts and feelings. Because you don't know the best way to manage your emotions and anxiety, it can make it really difficult to overcome anxiety.

4. External stressors

There are many external factors that can lead to anxiety, such as loss of job income or relationships. These events trigger the body to make cortisol, and other stress hormones. Although this is normal, it can often lead to excessive cortisol release over time. This can lead to anxiety symptoms.

5. Negative thinking is a part of everyday life

Negative thinking may cause isolation and loneliness that can further compound the problems mentioned.

6. Relationship problems

It is often difficult to know how to feel when your girlfriend or boyfriend is not around.

So much of your happiness will depend on that relationship. You can feel overwhelmed by your emotions if they aren't there.

7. Physical Health

The brain and the body are closely connected in many ways. When one feels unhappy, it can affect both mental and bodily. If the brain doesn't function properly, it can lead to anxiety or depression.

How to overcome your anxiety

1. Be free from negative thinking

We can feel happier if we view our lives from a positive angle.

2. Think positively

Positive thinking can be used to solve problems. One way is to visualize the outcome you desire, to choose positive thoughts based on how they feel. Another way is to think about all the options that will lead to positive results.

3. Practice developing self-love

Being more compassionate and sympathetic towards yourself. See your anxiety as a roadblock keeping you from becoming the person you desire to be.

4. Change your diet

Food choices can have a major impact on mental health. Certain foods may make you more anxious than others. As you become more aware of the impact your diet has on your physical health, you may be able to disconnect yourself.

5. Get help

You should seek support if you feel anxious.

6. Change your habits

Small changes in habits can make a big difference in your ability to feel calmer, less anxious and more relaxed. Establish good habits like getting enough sleep every night, being aware about sugar intake, exercising frequently (if possible), writing down anxiety attacks, taking powernaps, and having regular sleep/wake periods.

7. Change your environment

The environment where you spend your time can have a huge impact on how you feel. This resource provides some ideas for changing your living or work environment to make it more enjoyable. You might consider practicing yoga, walking, listening to music, and eliminating secondhand cigarette smoking.

8. Breathe

Deep belly breaths are one the best things you can do. It slows down your nervous system and helps reduce anxiety.

9. Take up yoga or meditate to cultivate mindfulness.

You can do it in the privacy and comfort of your bedroom with online sessions.

Case study: Exam anxiety

This case study discusses Richard's exam anxieties, their symptoms, and how they affected his performance in medical school. Finally it explains what Richard can do.

Richard was a dedicated medical student. He would feel intense anxiety when it came time to take exams. This would manifest itself in a racing heart, sweaty hands, and enormous concentration difficulties. Richard started to feel these symptoms. He became very anxious about his exam performance and began to attempt to kill himself to avoid the anxiety he had grown to love.

This fear prevented Richard from performing well on exams. He scored especially poorly in his finals. Richard began to worry about his future performance and was unable to get good grades. This problem plagued Richard for two years.

Although he was in medical school, it wasn't known if he ever suffered from anxiety or any related issues as an adult.

Richard found that he was unable to understand the reasons behind his feelings of depression and poor performance, even though he was a highly competent and intelligent medical student.

Richard's experience is not unusual among students who have experienced similar feelings at exam times. It is possible to help manage these symptoms by being aware of them and learning how to understand them.

Richard can ease his anxiety by focusing on the feeling and not trying to avoid it. Richard may also take deep breaths, look out of the window, or do relaxation exercises whenever he feels it.

www.ingramcontent.com/pod-product-compliance
Lightning Source LLC
Chambersburg PA
CBHW071221210326
41597CB00016B/1901